Lora,
PLEASE
ZIP
UP MY
ARMOR

MAB GRAFF HOOVER

Lord, PLEASE ZIP UP MY ARMOR

*E*very Working Woman
needs protection for:
her SPIRIT to protect her self-worth
her MIND to keep her from compromising
her HEART to enable her to resist temptation
her SOUL to protect her convictions

Daybreak Books

Zondervan Publishing House
Grand Rapids, Michigan

The incidents in this book are based on fact, but names have been changed.

Lord, Please Zip Up My Armor
© 1986 by Mab Graff Hoover

Daybreak Books are published by
Zondervan Publishing House
1415 Lake Drive, S.E.
Grand Rapids, Michigan 49506

Library of Congress Cataloging-in-Publication Date

Hoover, Mab Graff.
   Lord, please zip up my armor.

   Women—Prayer-books and devotions—English.
2. Hoover, Mab Graff. I. Title.
BV4844.H664   1986   242'.43   86-15955

ISBN 0-310-35641-5

Edited by Linda Vanderzalm
Designed by Julie Ashurman Linh

Printed in the United States of America

88   89   90   91   92   93   94 / EP / 10   9   8   7   6   5   4   3   2

CONTENTS

VAPOGAS INC PERSONNEL

President .... Mr. Archibald
   Secretary .... Valorie Vasquez
Traffic .... Mr. Rudd
   Secretary .... Myrna Dyer
Receptionist .... Mitzi McCormick
Head of Accounting .... Bob Tsuji
   Aid .... Betty Moore
Engineering .... Mr. Spencer
   Secretary .... Florine Hansen
Vice President/Propane . Mr. Ulrich
   Secretary .... Ellen Carter
Sales Manager .... John Beardsley
Floating Helper .... Mab
Extra Worker .... Rhoda

Vapogas Inc.

Parking

Lobby

| Pres. of Company MR. ARCHIBALD | VALORIE | Traffic MR. RUDD | MYRNA | | Switchboard Mailroom MITZI | Engineering MR. SPENCER | F L O R I N E | Head of Department MR. ULRICH |
| | | | | | | | | ELLEN |

						Women's Room	Supplies	
							MAB	Sales
					Conference-Cafeteria	C L O S E T		JOHN
Accounting BOB TSUJI	Drafting	Men's Room						

INTRODUCTION

If you're a woman and have to go outside your home to work everyday, this book is dedicated to you. I know how you feel when that hateful alarm clock goes off and you have to get up, even if a sick child or a barking dog has kept you awake most of the night. I've been there. I understand how you feel when you have to make sandwiches every morning and then find sacks to put them in and feed the baby and clean up the mess the puppy made—and all this before breakfast. I know how it is when you feel like being crabby, yet you must make the effort to appear reasonably sweet as you encourage your husband for his day. I know what it's like to paw through the closet, trying to find clothes that don't need pressing or mending or clothes that aren't too tight. I've been there as you drive through unbelievable traffic to get to the job site.

I sympathize with you when you come home so tired you wish you could just go to bed. You take off your dress of respect and equality and become mother-wife-servant again. You try to get the house in some semblance of a home. You have dinner to prepare. Kids to read to. Dishes to do. Clothes to wash. Babies to bathe. Love to make.

And then it starts all over again. . . .

I felt that it was important for you to know that I sympathize with you. But I believe it is much more important for you to know that Jesus sympathizes and loves you very much. I have found that when I turn to Him with any problem, He always gives a solution.

But we need to put on His armor. As my editor, Julie Link, puts it, "Working women need armor for their minds to keep them from compromising values to gain the acceptance of co-workers; and they need armor for their hearts to resist the temptation to put job responsibilities ahead of family responsibilities."

The Bible says, "So use every piece of God's armor to resist the enemy whenever he attacks, and when it is all over, you will still be standing up" (Ephesians 6:13, Living Bible).

My prayer is that this little book will help you put on that armor, and keep it on.

PROLOGUE

"Mother? Are you awake?"

"I am now."

"Can I turn on the light?"

"Sure. Hi, sweetie."

"Look!"

"Joanie! A diamond!"

"Isn't it beautiful? We want to get married next June."

"Oh! So soon?"

"It's almost a year—"

"But you still have two more years of college."

"We can handle it! Oh, mother, I'm so happy! I want to get married in our church and invite everyone we know!"

"Of course, but it'll cost a lot of money."

"I'll get a part-time job."

"It'll take more than that, sweetie—the flowers, the reception—"

"Don's mom will do the cake! Oh, mother, I've dreamed of walking down the aisle ever since I was a little girl."

"I know. And Lord willing, you will! Even if I have to go to work, too. I want you to have the wedding you've always dreamed of."

FUMBLE BEGINNINGS

"YOUR APPLICATION INDICATES you took one semester of art." Mr. Ulrich, Vice President in charge of Propane Division, looked at me through map-blue eyes, unblinking. Vapogas INC had hired me two weeks before as a floating secretary, and so far I'd gotten along all right. But I dreaded the times when Mr. Ulrich called me into his office because I couldn't always understand what he was talking about. He was a nice man and good-looking—tall, brown hair, nice mouth—but he was the vaguest, wordiest boss I'd ever worked for. He leaned forward. "Do you still practice your artistic expertise?"

I shrugged. "Sometimes." I tried to smile, but my upper lip felt as if a thread was pulling it up and down.

"Do you think you could execute a delineation that would agnately benefit the salespeople as they prevail against the resistance to standby installations?"

I blinked. He was speaking English, but what had he said? I bit the inside of my lip. "I guess I could try."

"Good!" He put my application aside and opened a catalog. He turned it around and pointed to a chart. "What we need is something homogeneous, yet something that will describe the convolutions, depressment, and gallonage versus expenditures, in sequence or approximate."

My lips compressed as I tried to understand. A knot was forming in my stomach. "I'm sure if you'll explain exactly what you want, I can draw it."

He went to the chalk board, made a few strokes down and across then labeled some of the columns. At last I discovered that (maybe) he wanted a comparison chart of costs, propane versus natural gas.

At the small desk they had assigned to me in the supply room, I studied the catalog chart, price lists, consumption graphs, and other figures he'd given me, and I shook my head. It was time for prayer.

Dear Lord, I need You to show me exactly how Mr. Ulrich wants this chart.

Jesus said, "Which of you, if his son asks for bread, will give him a stone?" (Matt. 7:9).

Thank You, Lord! I know You know every hair on my head, so I'm sure you know what's *in* Mr. Ulrich's head.

"We [I] have the *mind of Christ*" (1 Cor. 2:16, italics added).

LOOK BEFORE YOU WEEP

"I'VE HAD A ROUGH MORNING," I whispered to Florine, Mr. Spencer's secretary, in Engineering.

She was waiting for me to join her for lunch in the combination conference/dining room. Two young women from Accounting were seated at the opposite end of the table. My high heels clacked on the gray tile as I crossed to the tiny refrigerator the company provided for employees and took out my lunch.

"I saw you with Mr. U." Florine put out her cigarette. "Anything wrong?"

"I hope not. He wanted me to make up a chart the salespeople could use to help them demonstrate the savings they'd get by using standby systems—at least, I think that's what he wanted." I let out my breath and sat down beside her. "With all respect to him," I lowered my voice. "he isn't the best explainer in the world."

A smile quivered on one side of her mouth as she opened her lunch. She was too professional to say anything unkind about another employee, but the twinkle in her dark eyes said enough. I probably would have been fired the first week if it hadn't been for Florine's help, and I appreciated her.

She took a sip of tea. "Do you think it's okay?"

"The chart? I'd like you to look at it before I give it to him." I hunched my burning shoulders and sighed. *If I weren't working, I could take a nap this afternoon.* "Sometimes I wonder why I ever wanted this job!"

Her eyes widened. "I thought you wanted to work."

"I do—kind of. But now that I can't stay home, I remember how nice it was."

"Really? My husband wants me to stay home, but I'd go crazy." She bit into her sandwich and chewed thoroughly. "Do you have to work?"

I nodded. "Our daughter is getting married next June."

"Oh. Elegant weddings are expensive."

I frowned. "It's not going to be *elegant.*" Why was I on the defensive? Was it because Christians are supposed to be content with what they have?

She patted her lips with a napkin. "Anyway, I hope you're not going to quit. The company has two week's training invested in you."

"Oh, don't worry." I grinned. "I'll stay—'til I get fired! And when Mr. U. sees the chart, it might be today."

Lord, is it wrong for me to want Joan to have a lovely wedding? She's so sweet that I know she'd agree to a small one if I said so. But I want her to have what I didn't have!

"Keep your lives free from the love of money and be content with what you have" (Heb. 13:5).

But, Lord, wouldn't it be a bad testimony to quit this job now? You heard what Florine said. But I promise, in the future I'll try to get Your answer before I make a major decision.

"For the Lord gives wisdom, and from His mouth come knowledge and understanding" (Prov. 2:6).

ALL ONE BODY WE

"WHY IS THE MAIL DAMP?" I peeked in at my husband, sprawled on the couch, a letter in his hand. I turned the fire down under the hamburgers and went to the living room. "I don't think you want to know." He looked up at me. "Twinkie threw up on it."

"Yuk!" He dropped the letter to the floor.

"She couldn't help it." Our sweet old dog lifted her brown eyes to his and thumped her tail. "She got as close to the door as she could. She probably thought the mail under the drop was newspaper." My husband was pale. "Anyway, I washed it all off. That's why it's damp."

"Please! I don't want to hear anymore!" He closed his eyes for a moment. "What made her throw up?"

"Because *you* forgot to take out the trash. She ate all the fat I trimmed off the ham."

He took a pen from his shirt pocket and poked around in the junk mail. "Nothing important today, anyway."

"No, but I hope you'll remember the trash tomorrow morning." I gave him an imposed-upon look. "It wasn't fun for me to clean it up, after a hard day at work—" (Actually, the cleaning up hadn't been too bad. As any mother knows, raising children is excellent training in revolting cleanups.)

"I never used to have to take out the trash before you started work. Why can't the kids—"

"Honey, you know they have early classes, and they're both working afternoons—"

"What am I doing, loafing?"

I controlled an urge to stamp my foot. "Don't you remember when we had that meeting with the kids and decided who would do what? You said you'd rather take out the trash than unload the dishwasher."

"Okay, okay. I'll try to remember." He looked at the damp envelope and shivered. "But I think I'll put up an outside mailbox this weekend."

A lot of the hassles in this family could be avoided if we would all do our own jobs. We've got to work as *one*. . .

"For we were all baptized by one Spirit into one body" (1 Cor. 12:13a).

Oh, I understand what You're telling me, Lord! I've neglected some of my jobs in the church family since I started to work. Either I'm going to have to put out extra effort or find someone to take over some of the responsibilities. Otherwise Your work will suffer.

"If one part suffers, every part suffers with it" (1 Cor. 12:26).

TOO SMART IS DUMB

"YOU DID A GOOD JOB on that chart, Mab." Ellen Carter, Mr. Ulrich's secretary, smiled at me. Ellen was close to sixty, with thin dyed-black hair, black penciled eyebrows, and thin red lips. Behind thick glasses, her eyes seemed even larger than they were. Her tiny body was always fluttering, from files to computer to Mr. Ulrich's office, like a sparrow looking for food. I was in awe of her. She seemed to know everything about the liquid petroleum gas industry. I'm sure it was her brains that kept Mr. Ulrich in his high position.

Ellen flicked a light to her long cigarette. "I'm not going to worry at all while I'm in Portland, with you in charge."

My mouth opened. "In charge?"

"My mother's sick." She blew smoke from one side of her mouth. "I'll only be gone a week. You can hold the fort that long."

"But Mr. Ulrich—"

"He left yesterday for the gas convention in Dallas. He'll be gone until next Friday, too."

I glanced around her cluttered office with apprehension yet anticipation. In charge? Excitement began to build as I went back to my supply office. I could see myself seated at Ellen's desk! First, I'd tackle those "In" boxes and after that . . .

The following Monday evening my husband put his arm around me. "How come you're so blue tonight?"

"Oh, I sort of got in trouble today." It was hard to keep from crying.

"In trouble? What happened?"

"Well, you know Mr. Ulrich and Ellen were both gone last week and I was in charge?" He nodded. "A few things went wrong. Like one day when I was using the word processor, I was going to store a letter on the disk, but instead I erased a long contract."

"I thought those things were foolproof."

"They are if you think before you answer 'yes.' And then I rearranged Mr. Ulrich's catalogs by size and color—"

"You *what?*"

"That's what he said. But they looked much better!" I sniffed. "And I honestly didn't see what difference it would make, but Mr. Ulrich was really upset. Probably the worst thing that happened was I lost a customer."

"Oh, no! How?"

"This grouchy guy called and was bawling me out about some bid the company had made, and then mother called—see, Ellen has four lines—so I put him on hold, and then Florine called while I was talking to mother, and I just got mixed up."

"So?"

"I thought I was talking to mother and told her I couldn't talk long because some old grouch was on hold."

Lord, for one glorious week I thought I could do no wrong. Now I'm wondering if I can do anything right? Is there any way I can get back that customer?

"Do not think of yourself more highly than you ought, but rather think of yourself with sober judgment, in accordance with the measure of faith God has given you" (Rom. 12:3).

Forgive me, Jesus, for being so presumptuous and for hurting that customer's feelings.

"When pride comes, then comes disgrace, but with humility comes wisdom" (Prov. 11:2).

SORRY!

"MR. PRINGLE?" My heart was thudding so hard my chest hurt. "This is the—uh—secretary at Vapogas who—yes—wait! Please don't hang up!" Sweat popped out on my forehead. "I want to apologize for what I said yesterday. Sir—no, Mr. Ulrich doesn't even know I'm calling. It wasn't his fault. Please, Mr. Pringle—" My voice broke and tears dripped on the phone. "Please forgive me for calling you a—grouch!"

By lunchtime I still hadn't been fired, so I tiptoed into Mr. Ulrich's office and stood in front of his desk. After a long moment he looked up at me. His expression was as unreadable as blank paper.

"Mr. Ulrich, I want to apologize for rearranging your catalogs. And I'm so very sorry I lost a customer."

He put aside the trade journal he was reading and leaned back in his chair, his hands clasped across his stomach. His eyes were soft. "Mab, there are beneficial, ministerial, and sententious maxims in the Holy Scriptures. A favored jewel of mine is, 'All things work together for good.'" He winked for emphasis. "Mr. Pringle telephoned a few moments ago and indicated that his intentions have ameliorated somewhat toward Vapogas." I squinted at him as I tried to understand. Suddenly his smile lighted his face like sunrise in July, and in plain English he said, "We got the purchase order, baby."

Smiling, I backed out and turned toward Ellen's desk. I still had one more apology to make.

"Ellen, I feel awful about losing that file."

"Well, it's no skin off my nose!" She grinned. "You're the one who is going to have to feed it all back into the computer."

Calling Mr. Pringle and telling Mr. Ulrich and Ellen I was sorry were about the hardest things I've ever had to do. But there was no way out. Not only was I on the verge of losing my job, but my pride had already messed up my Christian testimony.

Lord, thank you for giving me courage to apologize. I really tried to get out of it, didn't I?

"Fools mock at making amends for sin" (Prov. 14:9a).

I feel so much better now that it's over.

Jesus said, "Settle matters quickly with your adversary" (Matt. 5:25a).

ONE SHEEP, TWO SHEEP—

IT'S 2:00 A.M. AND I'M SITTING on the couch in the living room. I haven't slept one minute this whole night! Once I was almost gone and the neighbor's dog began to bark. I thought about sneaking over there and opening the gate so he'd run away! I can't believe I had such a rotten thought. But he hasn't barked for hours, so why can't I sleep? I don't know what's wrong. I didn't drink coffee, and I'm not worried about anything—well, I'm a little anxious about tomorrow because I have to work in Accounting, and I've never helped out there before. Still, I don't think I'm worried enough about it to keep me awake.

Once when I was almost asleep, my dearly beloved began to snore. I thought about smacking a pillow on his face, but I remembered he told me I snore sometimes, too. I got up and came in here to watch TV, but all the programs seem dumb to me. Now I've eaten a bowl of cereal and a piece of toast, and I still can't sleep. Rats! I've got to get to sleep so I can be sharp in Accounting. Maybe if I read the Bible awhile I'll get sleepy. Wonder what it has to say about sleep?

The concordance lists "sleep," "sleeper," "sleeps." Hmm, it says here that Paul endured beatings, imprison ment, hard work, hunger, and sleepless nights (2 Cor. 6:5). Thank heavens at least I'm not in prison, I haven't been beaten, and I'm certainly not hungry. Or am I? Maybe another piece of toast.

Look at this, "So the Lord God caused man to fall into a deep sleep; and while he was sleeping, he took one of the man's ribs . . . and made a woman from the rib . . ." (Gen. 2:21–22). The Lord caused Adam to sleep! Dear Lord, please cause me to sleep. Yawn. I think I am getting sleepy. Here's a wonderful verse: "I will lie down and sleep in peace, for you alone, O Lord, make me dwell in safety." (Ps. 4:8).

Lord Jesus, I'm going back to bed now. Your Word says I'm safe, and I'm well and comfortable. Even if I can't sleep, I'm resting. And Lord, please forgive me for wanting to let that dog run away. Help me do a good job in Accounting. All things are in Your hands.

"He grants sleep to those He loves" (Ps. 127:2b).

Lord, I know you love me.

PIECE OF CAKE

WHEN THE ALARM WENT OFF, I was amazed to discover my insomnia was all gone! I felt pretty good, too, except I was cold. The temperature had been in the nineties the first two weeks in September, but this morning the house seemed icy.

At work, I was trying to find a place to hang up my blazer in the supply room when Ellen came in.

"Glad you're early, Mab. Bob Tsuji in Accounting wants to explain your duties before eight o'clock. He's a fanatic about his department starting on time." She looked at my jacket. "I suggest you put it back on. He keeps that department like an iceberg. Besides, it will help you look more professional. He's all business." She turned and flitted down the hall, past Sales, past Mr. Ulrich's office, then she turned left. Her heels clicked as she passed Engineering, the reception area and mail room, the main door, past the conference and dining area—with me right behind her. She nodded to Myrna in Traffic and to Valorie Vasquez, the President's secretary, then she made another left. Too soon we were in front of the door of the Accounting department, and I was breathless, partly from the fast walk but mostly from anxiety. I was already afraid of Bob Tsuji. I'd heard one woman in Accounting claim, "He runs the department as if he were a Marine sergeant." For about the hundredth time I wondered what I'd be doing. I'd only had one semester of bookkeeping, and what was that to an exacting accountant? For a terrifying moment I couldn't even remember if debit meant add or subtract.

"Good morning!" Bob Tsuji smiled cordially when Ellen introduced us. His almost black eyes were merry, and I relaxed slightly. I was about half an inch taller than he, but that didn't seem to bother him. He shook my hand and grinned wider. "Ready to go to work?" He spoke with a slight Oriental accent.

I bit my lip. "I just hope I can do the work."

When Ellen left us, he led me to a much bigger desk than the one in the supply room. "Don't worry. You can do the work." He grinned again. "Ellen says you're an excellent typist." He pointed to a new typewriter. "I just need you for a few days to get us caught up on typing."

My shoulders went limp with relief, and my grin matched his.

Thank you, Lord! I can type much better than I can calculate.

"Before they call I will answer; while they are still speaking, I will hear" (Isa. 65:24).

To think I stayed awake most of last night worrying! Will I ever learn to trust You completely?

Jesus said, "Therefore, do not worry about tomorrow" (Matt. 6:34a).

GLORY TO GOD!

THE ACCOUNTING DEPARTMENT was L-shaped. The longest part (called "the bull pen") was a room full of desks, calculators, and computers. The other part was Bob Tsuji's glass-enclosed office. Outside his cubicle were two desks, one on either side of his door. Mine was on the left. As I sat self-consciously, waiting for him to tell me what to do, a vivacious, plump woman bounced through the door, calling, "G-o-o-d morning!" She came to the desk across from mine and dropped a bulging, embroidered shopping bag on it. She jammed her purse in one of the drawers. "I'm Betty, and I'll bet you're Mab."

I smiled. "How did you know?"

"Great intellect!" She tipped her head back when she laughed, and I could almost see her tonsils. "No, I sent the memo to Mr. Ulrich for extra help, and he told me about you." So, she was evidently Bob's assistant. Other employees were taking their places and Betty became brisk. She handed me two file folders. "You'll start with these. We're so far behind." After she explained what she wanted me to do, she sat down and became absorbed in her own work.

I rolled a memo form into the new typewriter and began to feel for the "on" switch. I felt everywhere—underneath, on the sides, front, and back. This was ridiculous! I had typed on all kinds of machines. I stood up, leaned over, and studied the back.

"Something wrong?" Betty sounded impatient.

My face felt hot. "I can't turn it on."

She came over and jabbed the key labeled "power" on the keyboard, and immediately a red demon's eye glowed on the typewriter.

I felt like a complete fool. "Lord," I prayed silently, "please help me not to do anything else stupid! The Bible says that if I lack wisdom, I can ask You" (James 1:5).

"Do you have plans for lunch?" Betty's green eyes looked expectant.

"Is it lunchtime already?"

While we ate, Betty told me she was a "fundamental, born-again, Spirit-filled Christian." I told her I also believed in Christ. In a confidential tone she said, "People here don't give the Lord a thought! It's up to us to demonstrate His power." Her eyes were wide and intense as she grabbed a quick breath. "I believe our whole life— everything we do—should be toward the one goal of bringing glory to God."

For some reason I felt depressed.

She took a Bible out of her shopping bag and quoted: "Live such good lives among the pagans that, though they accuse you of doing wrong, they may see your good deeds and glorify God" (1 Peter 2:12). She stole a glance around the room and whispered, "We're among pagans!"

Lord, this is serious. What can I do to bring glory to You? I'm no preacher.

Jesus said, " . . . tell how much God has done for you" (Luke 8:39).

It's easy to praise You and give a testimony at prayer meeting, Lord, but I'm not sure I can do it here.

Jesus said, "If anyone is ashamed of me and my words, the Son of Man will be ashamed of him" (Luke 9:26a).

THE WAY THE COOK GRUMBLES

IN THE RESTAURANT LAST NIGHT my husband bit into his steak sandwich and looked mournful. "Do you know how long it's been since you made vegetable soup?"

"Hmm. Last winter?" I ventured. "So what?"

His mouth turned down. "Seems like it's been a year since I've had a home-cooked meal."

It most certainly had not been even a week since he'd had a home-cooked meal! We ate at his mother's last Sunday. I have to admit, though, that since I have started working, my home cooking has been pretty sketchy. Our meals consist mostly of Kentucky Fried Chicken, bacon and eggs, or hamburgers. I watch our vitamins, though, and occasionally try to have freshly boiled frozen vegetables, which nobody eats.

This morning I decided to cook a good meal for my family. It was Saturday, and I wanted to get that sad look off my husband's face. The menu would be:

Swiss steak

mashed potatoes and gravy

carrots and baby peas

Jell-O, fresh fruit

hot rolls

apple pie

At six o'clock I pushed a damp lock of hair off my forehead and yelled, "Dinner's ready!"

The table looked nice. It was the first time I'd used a tablecloth since Mother's Day. I went to the back door. "Hey! Dinner's on!"

When my husband came in, his face was pale. "Sorry. I didn't hear you the first time."

"If you didn't hear me the first time, how did you know I'd called twice?"

"Your tone gets edgy the second time."

"Where are the kids? This stuff is getting cold."

"Ron is gone to Barbara's. Don't know where Joan is."

"Here I am, mother, but I'm not eating." Joan patted her hips. "Gotta lose weight for my wedding!"

My husband sat down at the table. "I think I'm coming down with something. A little Jell-O is about all I can manage."

I looked at the loaded table. I was coming down with something, too. I could feel hot tears behind my eyes.

Lord! What's the use?

"Be patient and stand firm, because the Lord's coming is near. Don't grumble against each other . . . or you will be judged" (James 5:8–9a).

But all that work—and I hate to cook anyway!

"Let us not become weary in doing good . . . as we have opportunity, let us do good to all people, especially to those who belong to the family of believers" (Gal. 6:9–10).

(One good thing—this stuff should make pretty good soup.)

BUG-EYED? MAYBE

"I DON'T SEE YOU VERY MUCH since you've been working in Accounting." Florine brushed her short, auburn hair and smiled at me in the mirror.

"I know!" I put on lipstick and compressed my lips. "It's too bad we have to have a different lunch hour. But, I don't think I'm going to be there much longer."

"Oh?"

"Bob only needed me to help them get caught up on some things—mostly interoffice correspondence."

"No problems?" She gave me a wise look.

"I don't think so."

"That's good." She washed and dried her hands. "I know you were worried that you couldn't do the work."

"Worried isn't the word! Between what Ellen and some of the others had said about Bob, I was scared." I fluffed out the hair around my face. "But I needn't have worried. He's been nice to me. Anyway, Betty gives me my work."

The thought of Betty was slightly irritating, like a goad. She was such a holy Christian that she made me feel guilty. I looked directly at Florine in the mirror, and our eyes met. I felt blood rush to my cheeks. I'd known her for several weeks and had never said anything to her about my faith or church or Jesus Christ. Did silence glorify God?

"Also," my eyes looked scared, "I prayed." Florine looked startled. "I mean, it isn't just that Bob is nicer than

33

I thought or that I am so competent. I prayed that the Lord would help me do a good job."

Her eyebrows went up, and she smiled politely. She quickly put the strap of her bag over her shoulder and opened the restroom door. She looked back at me. "I've got to get back to my desk! See you later!"

I shrugged. At least I'd said something about the Lord.

I hate to have people think of me as a bug-eyed fanatic, Lord. Yet, I do love You. Thank You for giving me courage to speak.

Jesus said, "Tell them . . . how he has had mercy on you" (Mark 5:19b).

Florine probably thinks I'm peculiar, but I feel good!

"You will receive power when the Holy Spirit comes on you; and you will be my witnesses . . ." (Acts 1:8).

BLACK SLIP SHOWING

THIS MORNING MYRNA from traffic came around to take up a collection for Mitzi McCormick, the reception-ist. It was Mitzi's birthday, and the staff was giving her a party with cake and coffee about 3:00 P.M. in the conference room. I didn't know Mitzi very well. The only time I'd ever talked to her was the day I came for my interview, but everyone seemed to like her. She was pretty and looked a lot like Farrah Fawcett. She emphasized that look with her clothes and make-up. Men found excuses to hang around her tiny office, and she almost always had a male lunch date.

"She's married, too!" Betty "tsk-tsked" to me one day. "Has three children." She sighed and shook her head. "Pagans!"

When it was 3:00, Bob gave us permission to join the party. Almost everyone was there, even Mr. Ulrich. Mitzi was darling and appreciative. She got tears in her eyes when we sang "Happy Birthday" and acted like a little girl when she was handed the gift. Her eyes were big as she untied the ribbon and slipped off the wrapping paper. She took off the lid and gasped. "It's gorgeous!" She picked up a lacy, black half-slip from the box.

"There's more!" Myrna called.

Mitzi held up a black lace bra and bikini panties. All the men howled and whistled, and almost everyone was laughing. Somebody yelled, "Model 'em!" Then everyone began to clap.

Mitzi slammed them back in the box and ran from the room. There was a confused murmuring. Everyone looked puzzled and worried. Was she offended? Suddenly, Mitzi burst through the door again, smiling like the woman in a Close-up toothpaste ad. She'd put the panties and bra on over her tan slacks and blouse. Though she was completely covered, the effect was devastating. She danced seductively around the room, twirling the slip in her hand. Everyone went wild, except Betty, who jumped up and rushed out.

As I walked back to Accounting, Mitzi passed me, holding a paper plate with a piece of cake on it. She turned around and waved her slip as she trotted by in her black lingerie. "Our Prez couldn't get away for my party," she explained. "It'd be a shame for him to miss his cake."

What a character! Maybe Betty's right. And yet, before I was saved, I might have done the same thing—or worse.

Lord, thanks again for saving me and giving me new desires.

> **"What benefit did you reap at that time from the things you are now ashamed of? Those things result in death!" (Rom. 6:21).**

> **"Therefore, since Christ suffered in his body, arm yourselves also with the same attitude . . . he does not live for human desires, but rather the will of God. For you have spent enough time in the past doing what pagans choose to do" (1 Peter 4:1–3a).**

THINGS ALWAYS WORK OUT

SHORTLY AFTER MITZI'S BIRTHDAY PARTY, my work was finished in Accounting. I was glad. That department was too quiet for me. The only time I felt free to leave my desk was at lunch. Down at Mr. Ulrich's end of the building, however, there were plenty of reasons to move around, so it seemed like a homecoming to me the morning I again took up residence in the supply room. But it wasn't for long.

"Mitzi's going on vacation in two weeks," Ellen told me the first day I was back. "You'll have to learn her job."

"E-eek! That forty-button telephone thing?"

After lunch Mitzi pulled up a chair for me, and I began to learn her job. In the first couple of hours I realized why I'd need two weeks to learn everything she had to do. Besides taking all the calls, she sorted the mail, gave out applications, made appointments for interviews, and gave typing and shorthand tests. She met and screened all visitors and knew how to give a firm yet kind turndown.

I'd thought her behavior at her birthday party was pretty bizarre, but her everyday approach to the job was even more outrageous. She was rowdy, even naughty, with the men in Sales but a perfect lady with new customers and strangers. She was a clown, willing to hide her glamour for a laugh. While I was training, I found out why everyone loved her. For one thing, she was a good listener and seemed to understand problems and heartaches, from broken romances to rebellious children. I found myself telling her about wanting Joan to have a lovely wedding. "Yet I wonder if I am being materialistic?"

"I think every mother wants the best for her kids." She shook her head and bit her lower lip. "Man, that's why I'm working." Then she told me about her lawyer husband, in a wheel chair because of multiple sclerosis. "He's still working, but not much, and of course it's getting worse." Then she grinned and winked. "But what's that old saying about taking the bitter with the sweet? Things always work out."

I was amazed at her acceptance, serenity, even humor, in the midst of a tragic situation.

Mitzi may be a "pagan," but she handles adversity better than I do.

"When times are good, be happy; but when times are bad, consider: God has made the one as well as the other" (Eccl. 7:14).

Father, I know I'm not righteous, but because Jesus paid for my sins, You call me righteous. Help me to believe that You deliver me from all my troubles. Mitzi doesn't even know You, yet she believes things always work out.

"A righteous man may have many troubles, but the Lord delivers him from them all" (Ps. 34:19).

MS. PANTHER

I WAS AT MITZI'S RECEPTION DESK the day John Beardsley applied for a job in the Sales department. He was at least six feet tall, wide-shouldered and slim, splendid in a gray suit and white shirt. His eyes really looked like sapphires—dark blue and sparkling. His smile sparkled, too, setting off his tan. I peeked at him from time to time as he filled out the application. Later on that day I was pleased when he stopped by the desk and whispered, "I got the job!"

After Mitzi came back from vacation and I returned to my cubicle, I saw John quite often. The Sales department was just across the hall, and the salespeople were always in the supply room to get contracts and other forms or to have me type correspondence. I was always glad to see John. Everyone liked him.

"He's like a ray of sunshine," Florine said one day at lunch. "And he's so funny!" She tapped the side of her head. "And brilliant. Some of the salespeople offer the customers impossible deals that Engineering can't fulfill, but John always works them out with Mr. Spencer first."

"He's a good man," Ellen agreed. "I wouldn't be surprised to see him go up."

That afternoon Myrna from Traffic stopped at my desk. I quit typing and looked at her. "Hi. What's up?"

She reminded me of a smooth-running car. She was standing there in neutral, but her powerful engine was throbbing. She leaned down and whispered, "Were you on the reception desk when John Beardsley applied?"

"Uh-huh. Why?"

Her dark Italian eyes twinkled. "Is he married?"

I laughed. "Yep."

"Darn!" She frowned. "He doesn't wear a ring. Do you know how old he is?"

I shook my head. "I didn't read his ap. I just took him down to Mr. Ulrich."

"Can you get it?"

"Applications are locked up in Ellen's office. Ask her."

Myrna shook her head. "No. Ellen's a company person. She'd never bend the rules."

"Why do you want to know how old he is?"

"In case you hadn't noticed, he's a hunk!"

"But he's married."

"All's fair in love and war. Be a sweetie and try to find out how old he is. I wouldn't want to rob the cradle."

I watched her walk out the door, head held high, hips swaying. She was a gorgeous divorcee with two grown children.

There was a problem in John Beardsley's future.

Sudden fear turned my heart to ice. My fingers trembled as I put them on the keyboard. Was there a Myrna stalking my husband?

I don't think I could stand it if my beloved turned to someone else! I'm afraid. Lord, help me. Help us to stay in love.

"Have no fear of sudden disaster or of the ruin that overtakes the wicked, for the Lord will be your confidence" (Prov. 3:25–26a).

But You know, Lord, I'm not as young and beautiful as the women in his office.

"For this is the way the holy women of the past who put their hope in God used to make themselves beautiful. They were submissive to their own husbands . . . do not give way to fear" (1 Peter 3:5–6).

WHAT DAY IS WASH DAY?

"I'M OUT OF BLACK SOCKS!"

From the bathroom I could hear my husband thumping around in the bedroom. I looked up at the ceiling. Men! "Did you look in the top drawer?"

"Isn't that where the socks are kept?" His tone was as sour as lemon juice. "When did you wash clothes, anyway?"

I couldn't remember if I'd done a load Saturday or not. BVI (before Vapogas INC) I always washed every Monday and pressed on Tuesday. Now I tried to get everything done on Saturday, but I was always behind. I went to the bedroom and began to rummage through his sock drawer. "Do you have to wear black today?"

"Oh, no. I can just change my suit, shirt, and tie."

He was mad, and so was I. I mean, after all these years of having clean socks, would it kill him to get a pair out of the dirty clothes hamper once?

My chin jutted. "Anyway, I think I need a new washing machine."

"New! You don't use the one you have."

I slammed his drawer. "The reason you don't have any socks is because that machine is losing them." He glared at me and stepped out of his black pants into some brown ones. "I'm not kidding," I insisted. "I have a bagful of your socks that I can't match."

"Let me see that bag!"

I pulled it from under the bed and dumped out the socks. He snorted and mumbled while he tried to match up about twenty odd socks. At last he gave up. "See?" I gloated. "Now, don't you think I need a new washing machine?"

He put on his brown sports jacket then looked at me. "I think you need to remember you have a family!"

Well, lah-dee-dah! Sometimes I wish I didn't have a family!

I'm sorry, Lord. I don't mean that. But am I supposed to give up my goals over a pair of socks?

"A wife of noble character . . . watches over the affairs of her household" (Prov. 31:10a, 27a).

And that same wife in Proverbs worked to earn extra money, too (v. 16). So, I think I understand what You're telling me, Lord. Just because I've chosen to earn money for Joan's wedding doesn't give me the right to neglect my family. But there's not enough time!

"The wise heart will know the proper time and procedure. For there is a proper time and procedure for every matter" (Eccl. 8:5b—6a).

CURTAIN CAPER

I'VE BEEN TRYING TO "watch over the affairs of my household" since the squabble over the black socks. I've forced myself to be more disciplined about time, too. I don't sit in front of the TV for an hour after dinner watching the news anymore. I can hear it on the car radio on the way home, and they say the same thing over and over anyway. In that hour, with Joanie's help, I clean up the kitchen, make my sandwich, and usually do a load of clothes. My darling husband says the dryer interferes with TV reception, but I reminded him that his drawer is full of socks.

One evening a week I try to do a little extra to the house. For example, I hadn't realized how drab and dingy the kitchen curtains had gotten since I went to work.

On the way home one night, I bought some "Antique Gold" dye. That would certainly brighten up those curtains.

"Don't waste your time trying to dye them," you-know-who cautioned. "It'll just be a mess. Buy new ones."

"Don't worry!" I pooh-poohed. "I've dyed things before."

I followed the instructions to the letter and could barely wait for the washer to spin the last cycle. When I opened the lid, I choked at the sight of the mottled mess of mustard yellow with dots of something that looked like catsup.

44

"What happened?" Joan looked horrified.

"I haven't any idea." I felt tears pushing on my eyeballs. I leaned against the dryer and had an internal fit. All that time wasted on a stupid project. Joan's presence and my husband within earshot kept me from screaming and stamping the curtains to death. I got some satisfaction out of wadding them up and throwing them in the trash.

Forcing a note of cheer in my voice, I called, "Honey, I think maybe you're right. I'll just buy some new curtains tomorrow night."

These new white curtains are darling! And if I do get tired of the white, I can always dye them.

Lord, why did that happen? I thought dyeing the curtains would show how much I love my home.

"All a man's ways seem innocent to him, but motives are weighed by the Lord" (Prov. 16:2).

Motives? That's the answer! There's nothing wrong with dyeing curtains, but my motive—be honest, Mab,—was to make my husband notice how hard I was working.

"The Lord searches every heart and understands every motive behind the thoughts" (1 Chron. 28:9b).

TEMPTATION

ONE MORNING a few days after the curtains "dyed," I told Mitzi about it and we both laughed at my folly.

"Oh, we working wives do have our problems, don't we?" She laughed again then looked serious. "I have a real problem right now. I've gained five pounds, and it's not even Christmas yet!"

"Me, too! When I was home, I used to do most of the yard work. Now I don't exercise much, and I just don't have the incentive to diet."

She snapped her fingers. "I've got an idea." She leaned over and pulled a bathroom scale from under her desk. "Let's weigh ourselves and then see which of us loses the most weight by next week. Loser has to take the other one to lunch!"

"Can I play?" We both whirled around. John Beardsley was smiling at us. "Eating on an expense account has sure put some pounds on me!"

The next Monday morning John and I went to Mitzi's office, but she wasn't there. I began to take calls, and one of them was Mitzi. "My husband is sick. I'll call later." She hung up.

I looked at John. "Poor Mitzi."

"We could still weigh in."

"I really dieted this week." I pulled out the scale and stepped on. "Oh, good! I've lost three pounds!"

John stepped on it and grimaced. "Only one pound. Well, at least I get to take you to lunch." I felt a pinprick of danger.

But nothing happened at the restaurant. We talked a little about our spouses and children, but mostly we were self-consciously silent. When he paid the check, his arm accidentally bumped mine, and my heart dropped. I thought of him all afternoon.

That night when my husband kissed me, I wondered what John's kisses would be like, and immediately my heart ached with guilt.

After the dishes were done, I went to the living room and sat on the arm of my husband's chair. I kissed the top of his head. "I'm going to bed. I don't feel—like myself."

In bed my hands were sweaty as I fingered the Bible.

Lord! I need Your help! I haven't done anything, but I feel so guilty!

"Flee the evil desires of youth, and pursue righteousness . . ." (2 Tim. 2:22a).

How can I flee? I see John every day. Help me, Lord, to pursue righteousness. Get him out of my mind.

"She [Potiphar's wife] caught him [Joseph] by his cloak and said, 'Come to bed with me!' But he left his cloak in her hand and ran out of the house" (Gen. 39:12).

Lord, I promise You I will stay away from him. But please, make him stay away from me.

CHICKEN

"WHEN I STARTED BACK TO WORK," I complained to my husband, "I thought I'd get away from Avon, Amway, and Tupperware, but I have more people at work pester me than I ever had at home."

"You're kidding. Well, you don't have to buy. None of that stuff is any good, anyway."

I handed him a colorful brochure. "I think most of it's good. It's just that it usually costs more than the same thing in a store."

"All the more reason to say no. You're too easy."

"It's pretty hard to say no when they're friends."

"I wouldn't call them friends. They're using the office to put you on the spot."

"No, they're not! They're just like me, trying to make extra money. And when you look at these catalogs, it's hard not to order."

"It wouldn't be hard for me. I like to see what I buy."

"Look at these pictures. Don't they look—"

"You're hopeless. You'd better be careful with your money or you won't have enough for Joan's wedding."

I knew my husband was right. I am too soft. I've got to get tough. When I take these catalogs back Monday, I'll just say, "Sorry, not interested."

Several days later my husband took a big carton out of my arms, "Here, let me help you. What's this?"

"Christmas presents."

"It says 'Tupperware.'" He looked in the box. "Oh, no. It *is* Tupperware! And shaving lotion, perfume, soap—*rust remover?*"

"They *are* Christmas presents." He looked as if I'd just told him I was going to run for Miss America. I scowled at him. "These women need some extra money, and—" I tried to sound enthusiastic. "—and I need to buy Christmas presents, right? So—?"

"So don't give me the shaving lotion."

I slapped the flaps on the box together. He *would* have to see that.

He raised an eyebrow and grinned. "What a thrill for the giftee who gets the rust remover."

Lord, why am I such a chicken? I really didn't want to buy that stuff. If I'm completely honest, I have to admit that I want everybody to like me, and I'm afraid they won't if I don't buy.

"Fear of man will prove to be a snare, but whoever trusts in the Lord is kept safe" (Prov. 29:25).

Lord, develop my trust and help me become a stronger person.

"The Spirit helps us in our weakness. We do not know what we ought to pray, but the Spirit Himself intercedes for us . . ." (Rom. 8:26).

THE INVITATION

THE PRESIDENT'S SECRETARY SELDOM came to our end of the building, but one cold morning early in December, Valorie Vasquez quickstepped into Ellen's office. Her black hair bounced around her shoulders, and her dark eyes were smiling. "Good morning, you two." Her slight Mexican accent made her words go up and down in musical tones. "How's the world treating you?"

I smiled at her, but Ellen frowned at the papers in Valorie's hand. "What's Mr. Archibald up to now?"

Valorie laughed, a rich bubbling sound. "Notheeng bad, I can assure you." She gave us each a memo from him. "And here's a copy for Mr. Ulrich, okay?" She smiled and winked as she whirled around and left the office.

We both read the memo silently: "You and a companion are cordially invited to my home Friday evening, December 20th, for dinner and a Christmas party. Cocktails at 7:00, dinner at 8:00, party 9:00–?" The address was in Alhambra.

"Well, what do you know." Ellen put a king-size cigarette between her lips and lit it, although one cigarette was smoldering in the ashtray. "This is a first."

"Wow. If he invites everyone and a companion, there'll be a hundred people! How can he serve that many?"

"I've never seen his home, but Mr. Ulrich says it's a mansion. I'm sure there's plenty of room." She smiled crookedly. "Free liquor! Should be quite a bash."

I looked down at the invitation and worried. First of all, I didn't drink, and I hated to be around people who were drinking. Second, my husband probably wouldn't want to go, and third, would John Beardsley be there? My heart began to race. I hadn't seen him since we went to lunch, but there had been very few moments he hadn't been in my mind.

"Guess I'll get a new dress for the occasion." Ellen exhaled smoke through a dreamy smile.

"I don't think I'll go."

She jerked around to stare at me.

"Not go!" She shook her head. "Where do you plan to look for a job?"

I don't want to go, Lord, but Ellen practically said I'd lose my job if I don't, and I'm a long way from paying for Joan's wedding.

"Let not my heart be drawn to what is evil, to take part in wicked deeds with men who are evildoers; let me not eat of their delicacies" (Ps. 141:4).

Lord, what should I do? Maybe I'll get the flu.

"Blessed is the man who does not walk in the counsel of the wicked" (Ps. 1:1).

ORGANIZATION

DINNER WAS OVER AND I BEGAN to clear the table. I leaned down and kissed my husband on the cheek. "You know, honey, I'm surprised you want to go to Mr. Archibald's party."

"Why?" He looked up at me. "I'm always ready to get a free meal." He got up and followed me into the kitchen. "Anyway, I thought you wanted to go."

"I didn't say I wanted to go. It's just that Ellen seemed to think it was important." I sighed as I rinsed the dishes. "I was hoping you'd say no."

"Oh, come on. When will we ever get another chance to have dinner in a mansion?" I stiffened when he hugged me. "How come you're so grumpy?"

Sudden tears flooded my eyes. I wasn't sure why I felt grumpy. I turned to face him. "Probably because Christmas will be here in two weeks, and I haven't finished addressing Christmas cards, and I can't find a gift for mother, and I haven't wrapped anything I've bought!"

He hugged me to his chest. "Poor baby!"

"I don't have time to go to a dumb party!"

"There, there, sweetie. I'll help you."

I looked up at him. He'd never been very good help around the house, even when the kids were little. "You'll help me?"

"Sure. I'll help you get organized."

He led me to the couch and pulled me down beside him. "Now, it's obvious you can't do any shopping tonight. So, think. What can we do?"

I looked into his compassionate eyes. He really wanted to help. "Well, I can address cards while you load the dishwasher."

He frowned. "Where's Joan?"

"She and Don have gone to a game."

"Hmm. Okay, you can address cards tonight."

It was after midnight when I finally cleaned up the kitchen. The rat. I was sure he said he'd help, but bless his heart, I guess he did help, because the Christmas cards are ready to mail.

Lord, why do I still feel grumpy this morning? I thought Christmas was the season to be jolly.

> **"Do not be anxious . . . present your requests to God. And the peace of God, which transcends all understanding, will guard your hearts and your minds in Christ Jesus" (Phil. 4:6–7).**

Lord, I can't help but be anxious about that party—or rather about John Beardsley.

> **Jesus said, "Simon, Simon, Satan has asked to sift you as wheat. But I have prayed for you, Simon, that your faith may not fail" (Luke 22:31–32a).**

Are You praying for *me*, Lord?

CHRISTMAS PARTY

MY SISTER LOANED ME A DRESS for the Christmas dinner. It was a champagne-colored taffeta, with black velvet collar, buttons, and wide belt. "You look beautiful!" she declared when I tried it on. I felt beautiful the night of the party, but I was shaking with dread and excitement when we walked up the cement steps from the street level to the wrought-iron gate of Mr. Archibald's mansion. Every window was aglow, upstairs and down, and the front yard sparkled with Christmas lights on the trees leading to the double-sized front door.

We were greeted by a maid. I quickly gave her my old black coat before anyone else could see it. I waved to Florine across the room and moved toward her. We introduced our husbands, then I looked around. The spacious drawing room was filled with smoke, noise, and people. Mitzi was there, gorgeous in a black dress, and I wondered if she was wearing her black lingerie. Bob Tsuji, Ellen, Myrna—everyone seemed to be there, laughing, drinking, and having a good time. But where was John? Suddenly, a circle of people burst into loud laughter, some of them stepped back, and there he was, more handsome than ever. He was laughing, too, but when he saw me, his laughter faded. There was no mistaking the message his eyes sent. I thought my heart would stop.

After the elaborate buffet dinner was over (and Ellen had been right—there was plenty of room), waiters put the tables away and moved back the chairs. A five-piece band began to play. The music was exciting, and soon couples were whirling around on the hardwood floor in the sun room.

John came toward us, his face flushed and smiling. I introduced my husband. They shook hands, then with old-fashioned grace John asked, "May I dance with your wife?"

"Sure! Go ahead!"

John put his arm around my waist, and I immediately became rigid with self-consciousness. "I'm really not a very good dancer."

"Doesn't matter." He didn't sound like himself, and his breath smelled like liquor. "Been wantin' to hold you like this." He pulled me tight.

"John!" I pushed away.

He held me even tighter, forcing me to move with his dance steps. "Know you want me, too."

His breath sickened me. I stopped and pushed hard against his chest. I looked up into his inflamed eyes. "John, let go!" I frowned at him. "I'm a Christian—and I'm *married.*" I turned and started back toward my husband. Evidently to save face, John followed me.

My husband stood up and smiled at us. "Back so soon?"

"Thank you, very much," John said, bowing low.

"What was that all about?" my husband whispered.

I shrugged and mouthed the words, "He's had too much to drink."

It's over! The insane infatuation is over. Thank You, Lord, for a wonderful Christmas present. Now I know why you wanted me to come to the party. You wanted me to see that John doesn't compare to my husband.

"For you have been my refuge, a strong tower against the foe" (Ps. 61:3).

What a narrow escape! How can I keep from falling into a situation like that again?

"We must pay more careful attention, therefore, to what we have heard, so that we do not drift away" (Heb. 2:1).

TRADITION

"MOTHER!" JOAN RUSHED into the kitchen after church. "Do you realize one week from tonight is Christmas Eve?" Her shining eyes reminded me of when she was a little girl. "And you haven't made fruit cake yet."

"I don't think I will this year." I put the overdone chuck roast on a platter. "I just don't have time."

"But fruit cake is one of our traditions!"

After dinner while my husband was napping and Joan was studying, I got out the recipe for Blue Ribbon Fruit Cake. I knew I didn't have the time or all the ingredients, and Something whispered, "Don't try it." But Joan wanted fruit cake. I'm good at improvising, I told myself.

The first ingredient was white syrup; of course I didn't have any. But I did have molasses. Fortunately, I'd already bought candied fruit, but I didn't have orange citron. No problem. Candy orange slices would be just as good. I didn't know what to use for peach brandy until I found some peach jam that I had hidden from myself when I was dieting. There was one box of raisins (not enough) and no dates, but I did have a big bowl of stewed prunes and a can of fruit cocktail. No pecans? Well, salted peanuts would have to do.

By four o'clock, two loaf pans and three one-pound coffee cans were almost full of lumpy batter, cooking in a slow oven. "I can't go to church tonight," I told my husband when he woke up. "Have to tend to my cooking."

Three hours later I took the cakes out of the oven. While I was cleaning up the kitchen, my husband cut into one and immediately grabbed a spoon. "I didn't know you were making pudding." Mesmerized, I watched him dip into the sticky stuff.

"But it's not pudding!" Wet prunes and fruit cocktail had been a terrible mistake.

"It's good. What is it?"

"Raw cake!" There was nothing to do but grease all the pans and put the puddings back in the oven until they turned to cake.

Lord, was that You telling me not to mess with fruitcake this year? I guess I should have listened.

"Whether you turn to the right or to the left, your ears will hear a voice behind you saying, 'This is the way . . .' " (Isa. 30:21).

Lord, there *was* a bright side. Joan thought my "Innovative Fruit Cake" was the best I'd ever made!

JEHOVAH-JIREH

"WHEN MILLIE TOLD ME what she paid for Sandi's wedding dress," I said to Joan, "I about fainted." We'd been shopping for Joan's dress off and on for months, but now that the holidays were over, we knew we had to get serious. I really *felt* serious as we drove toward the mall. Worried was the word. "Honey, there's no way I can spend that much for your dress. That's almost as much as I've saved for the whole wedding." Joan's worried expression broke my heart. I reached over and squeezed her hand. "But I prayed before we left home tonight that the Lord would lead us to just the right store."

We parked in front of May Company. "We can start here," I said. In the bridal shop we both felt more dismal than ever. The prices were even higher than they had been before the holidays. "We'd better move on," I whispered and took Joan's arm.

A clerk stepped out from behind the counter. "May I help you?"

I gave her a hopeless half-smile. "I'm afraid not. These prices are a little rich for my blood."

She smiled at Joan. "Before you leave, let me show you something."

She took us back to the fitting rooms and brought out a bouffant, snowy creation of Chantilly lace and net over taffeta. It was trimmed with tiny seed pearls. Joan drew in her breath. "Oh, mother!"

"How much is it?" I tried not to care.

"Why don't we just try it on."

The sight of my baby in a wedding dress made me gasp. She was gorgeous, and the dress fit perfectly. "How much?" My voice sounded almost reverent.

"Well, it's last year's model." She raised her eyebrows. "It was twice this much last spring." She showed me the marked-down ticket, and I gasped again. Forty dollars less than the amount I'd set!

Thank You, Lord, for the new wedding dress Joan has hanging in her closet.

> **"And Abraham called the name of that place Jehovah-jireh [the Lord will provide]" (Gen. 22:14a KJV).**

Dear Lord, how can I thank You for hearing my prayer?

> **"Cast all your anxiety on him because He cares for you" (1 Peter 5:7).**

All? Are you sure, Lord. . . ? We still need invitations, food, flowers, a tux for Ron and daddy, and a dress for me.

HEAVENS!

"YOU'D BETTER LEAVE a few minutes early," my husband called out when he left for work. "The fog is pretty thick."

I got to work twenty minutes early and went to the lunchroom. Florine and Ellen were seated at the long table, smoking and reading the morning paper. I got a cup of coffee and sat down with them.

"What's a five-letter word for mountains?" Ellen asked.

"How about range?" Florine answered. "Hey! Listen to my horoscope for today: 'This is the day to invest, to make decisions, and to mend fences.' How amazing! I've been wondering whether or not to have the kitchen redone!" Her eyes were sparkling when she looked up. "I'm going to call those remodelers this morning!"

My mouth opened slightly. "Because of what you just read?"

"Of course." She looked imperious. "I wouldn't do anything really important without consulting my horoscope. Would you, Ellen?"

Ellen finished printing a word on the puzzle. "Well, I wouldn't go that far. But I do think the moon and stars have a bearing on our lives."

I sipped my coffee. I didn't believe in astrology. I remembered a sermon in which the preacher said, "Astronomy is a science, but astrology is a form of divination.

You can always tell the difference because astrology has an *L* in it—makes it rhyme with hell!" I had laughed at the time, but today I felt sad to realize that these two intelligent, mature women turned for advice to an astrologer's opinions in a newspaper.

Father, give me the courage to tell Ellen and Florine that You will help them and that You know all the answers.

"Let your astrologers come forward, those stargazers who make predictions month by month . . . Surely they are like stubble; the fire will burn them up" (Isa. 47:13b–14a).

Thank You for good Bible preachers who set me straight on all kinds of divination. Help me pass it on.

"They exchanged the truth of God for a lie, and worshiped and served created things rather than the Creator" (Rom. 1:25a).

Lord, how much more reasonable and reliable to get advice from You, the *Maker* of the moon and stars.

LIGHTS OUT

AFTER WORK I WAS STILL trying to think of a tactful way to talk to Florine and Ellen about the Lord, but they were so sure of themselves and not interested in Him. I got in my car, put the key in the ignition, and turned it. Nothing. Panic! It was almost dark, and nearly all the cars in the lot were gone. I twisted the key again, but there was only a hopeless click. I leaped out of the car and ran back to the building. Maybe—please, Lord—my husband hasn't gone home yet. Ellen was just leaving when I rushed back in. "Gotta use the phone!" She waited while I dialed. What would I do if he didn't answer?

"Hello?"

(Oh, thank You, Lord!) "Honey, the dumb car won't start," my voice sounded reproachful.

"What did you do?"

I stamped my foot. "I didn't do anything! The battery must be worn out."

"Can't be. We got it just before Thanksgiving, remember?" I nodded my head like a child talking on the phone. "So you must have done—"

"I did not do anything!" He made me so mad!

He sighed. "Well, it'll be another half-hour before I can swing by. I'll be there as soon as I can."

"I can take you home," Ellen offered when I hung up.

I gave her a bleak smile. "Thanks, but he's coming. The turkey! He always blames me!"

"I know!" Ellen grinned. "It's the nature of the beasts."

I started to walk outside with her, but it was too cold to wait in the car, and the fog was coming back in. I started to go to the women's room, but with everyone gone it was scary. I could hear thumping at the other end of the building and hoped it was the janitor. It was a long half-hour before my husband turned into the parking lot.

Shivering beside him, I watched as he opened the hood and tested the battery. "Hmm, it *is* dead. Wonder how come?"

"I don't know, but I know it's not my fault."

He got in the driver's seat, looked, and felt around a moment, then he snorted. In the pale glow from the building lights, I could see sarcasm on his face. "No wonder! You left the lights on all day!"

Oh, Lord. Just when I'm beginning to think I'm a capable, reliable, career woman, I do something dopey.

"The man who thinks he knows something does not yet know as he ought to know" (1 Cor. 8:2).

Lord, I feel like hating men! I'd like to get even, yet I know I'm wrong! G-r-r-r!

Jesus said, "Come to me . . . I will give you rest . . . learn from me, for I am gentle and humble in heart" (Matt. 11:28–29a).

TRADE SHOW

ELLEN POKED HER HEAD into the supply room. "Mr. U. wants to see you right away." Now what? I put on my jacket and trotted after her. Mr. Ulrich looked up when I opened his door.

"Good morning! My, you're looking splendorous!" He motioned at the chair by his desk. "Please, be seated." As I perched uneasily, I noticed brochures and drawings on his desk. "My dear, have you ever frequented a market hall?"

I stared at him while I translated. "Do you mean a trade show?" He nodded over peaked fingertips. "Yes, I went to the RV show in Anaheim last year."

"And did you observe the multitudinous compartments in which the representatives were housed?" I frowned. All I could remember about that day was how my feet hurt. He patted my hand. "Inconsequential." He handed me the drawings and brochures. "Peruse these a moment." They were sketches and pictures of trade booths, with bunting, literature, equipment, etc. I looked up at him. What was he building up to? "In February the Western Association of Liquid Petroleum Gas Dealers will be displaying their products at the Los Angeles Convention Center." He leaned back and folded his hands across his small pot belly. "I have selected you to work with a representative from Sales, not only to embellish Vapogas INC's enclosure but also to staff it those three days."

My eyes widened and I struggled to keep from smiling. "Me? Why?"

"Because of your demeanor, virtuosity, and dexterity—and also because I can't spare anyone else."

"Oh." Oh, well. I love to decorate, and those days downtown should be fun. To think I'll get paid for it, too. But wait! Didn't he say I would be working with someone from Sales?

Oh, please, Lord! Not John Beardsley.

"Those who live according to the sinful nature have their minds set on what that nature desires; but those who live in accordance with the Spirit have their minds set on what the Spirit desires" (Rom. 8:5).

The phrase "minds set" appears twice in this verse. If I set a cup down on my desk, it stays there until I pick it up. Lord Jesus, this moment, I *set* my mind on You.

LOOSE LIPS

ALONE IN THE LUNCHROOM, I began to study a library book about festival decorating when Betty from Accounting came in. "Hi," I said. "I haven't seen you for ages."

She dropped her shopping bag on the table and shook her head wearily. "It's tax time. Everything has to be done."

I tore off a piece of paper napkin, put it in the book, and closed it. "Come to think of it, I didn't even see you at Mr. Archibald's Christmas party.

She snorted and rolled her eyes like a wild horse. "I wouldn't be caught dead at a pagan affair like that." She bit her tuna sandwich angrily. "What if the Lord had come that night? I wouldn't want Him to look for me at a pagan brawl."

"Well, there was some drinking, but—"

"Oh, I know what the world does! The Bible tells us to 'come out from among them and be ye separate!' "

I opened a container of yogurt and stirred it. I hadn't wanted to go to the dumb party either. At least Betty was courageous enough to put her job on the line for her beliefs. Just the same, this woman was like having a sore toe in new shoes. I finished the yogurt as quickly as I could. "Guess I'd better get back."

When I went to get the mail after lunch, Mitzi motioned for me to come over to see something. I knew by her wild eyes that it had to be funny and probably even naughty. I sat down on a stool near her desk, and she gave me an envelope of pictures.

"They're of the Christmas party. Just got 'em back."

Taken after my husband and I went home, they were decidedly funny and naughty. I couldn't help but laugh, especially at one in which Mr. Ulrich had pulled up his pants above his knees and was posing like a bathing beauty. I thought of Betty. "Looks like a truly pagan affair." I flicked a wise glance at Mitzi. "Pagan. Betty's favorite word."

She laughed. "That woman! She needs a pulpit."

"Right." I stood up and stretched out my arms. "Come unto me, all ye pagans!"

We both howled, and when I turned to go, there stood Betty.

How long had she been there? How much had she heard? Whose side am I on, anyway? Why do I do these things?

I could only simper as I squeezed by her with the mail.

Lord, I feel so dirty. I know you've forgiven me, but I'll never forget how miserable I felt when I saw her.

"A man who lacks judgment derides his neighbor, but a man of understanding holds his tongue" (Prov. 11:12).

I've just read the twelfth chapter of Romans, and I confess, I don't even like Betty, much less love her. But she and I are family. I need You, Lord, to fill me with Your love.

"In Christ we who are many form one body . . . Be devoted to one another in brotherly love" (Rom. 12:5, 10a).

BEG PARDON

FOR TWO DAYS I KEPT TELLING THE LORD I was sorry for talking about Betty behind her back. Not only had I gossiped and been unkind, even sacrilegious, but I had talked against a Christian to a non-Christian. Yet no matter how many times I told Him I was sorry, I couldn't get relief. I knew I was going to have to get it straight with Betty.

In my mind I went over and over what I would say and her possible reactions—tears? anger? disdain? My heart pounded with fear. Getting up courage to talk to her was as hard, maybe harder, than the time I had to apologize to Mr. Pringle, Mr. Ulrich, and Ellen. What a source of pain my mouth has always been!

At last I dialed Betty's extension and made a date with her for lunch. "It's so warm," I suggested, "let's take our lunches out by those bushes in the side yard." I didn't want anyone to hear me eat crow.

We spread our sweaters on the lawn, and after she asked a long blessing, in which she beseeched the Lord to make the people at Vapogas INC repent, she began a monologue about her church, her family, and her job. When she finally quit talking long enough for me to start, I jumped right in.

"Betty, you know the other day when I was in the mail room with Mitzi?" My lips quivered and my armpits felt wet. "Well, I want you to know how sorry I am for talking like that."

She looked puzzled for a moment. Then she brightened. "Oh, you mean when you were imitating one of those lady preachers? Hey, I'm right with you! I don't believe in woman preachers either." She took a deep breath, and I could almost see her climbing up on the soapbox. "Christians don't study the Word!" Her expression was sorrowful. "You and I know the Bible says that women are not to usurp the authority of the man—First Timothy two and twelve!" She patted my hand. "But it's so good to know I can share these heartaches with a fellow believer."

Lord, I really felt like a toad. You not only protected me from a negative reaction, but You also protected her from hurt feelings. I can't believe she didn't realize I was making fun of her! Oh, thank You, Lord.

"Praise be to the Lord, for he showed His wonderful love to me" (Ps. 31:21a).

I'm a poor Christian. In Your strength, dear Lord, I hope I never again talk about people behind their backs.

"Set a guard over my mouth, O Lord; keep watch over the door of my lips" (Ps. 141:3).

GIRL THURSDAY

WHEN I PASSED ELLEN'S OFFICE this morning, I saw a woman seated by Mr. Ulrich's door. I didn't get a good look, but my impression was "dumpy and unkempt." At my desk I dialed Ellen's extension. Forgetting my manners, I pried, "Who's that?"

She was silent for a moment. Then she said, "Your timing is off."

"Can't talk, huh?" I giggled. It was fun to tease Ellen.

"You're a character. I'll be over." In a moment she appeared at my desk. "I really should make you sweat," she said, "but for your information, the woman's name is Rhoda Wilson, and Mr. U. is hiring her to do your work."

I blinked. "I'm fired?"

"No, dopey!" She lit a cigarette and coughed. "Someone has to do your work while you're downtown. Besides, since we landed the Indiana Glass contract, Florine is going to need help." She turned to go. "I'll bring Rhoda over pretty soon, nosy. You can show her the ropes."

"Where will she sit?"

"There's a table in Florine's office."

As I began to teach Rhoda my job, I felt we might have problems. First of all, she *was* unkempt. Her short dark hair was greasy, and she definitely had a body odor. Besides that, she was a chain smoker. But I could put up with all that. It was her know-it-all attitude that might cause problems. Examples:

"It's stupid to go to Florine for purchase order numbers. You should have them at your desk."

"Why make three copies? Clutters up the files."

"This dumb place doesn't even have a Coke machine. And they could be sued for making you work in this dungeon."

"You don't need to show me. I've done all this stuff before."

What an unpleasant person! Why did I get stuck working with her, Lord?

"Do not be surprised at the painful trial you are suffering, as though something strange were happening to you. But rejoice that you participate in the sufferings of Christ" (1 Peter 4:12−13a).

I know You had to work with some unpleasant people, too, Lord, but Rhoda is something else!

"I have learned to be content whatever the circumstances" (Phil. 4:11).

Whoops! I haven't learned that yet. I've got a feeling that between Rhoda and the Holy Spirit, I'm in for some rough tutoring.

STICKY FINGERS

ABOUT A WEEK AFTER RHODA WAS HIRED, Florine asked us if we'd like to shop for groceries with her during lunch. "For every roll of Scott Towels you buy at Keenes Market, you get one free!"

On the way, Florine and Ellen sat in the front seat and talked business, while in the back, Rhoda spoke softly to me. "Are you going to buy paper towels?"

I nodded quickly. "You bet! We really go through that stuff at our house."

She blew a cloud of smoke toward me and I choked. With three smoking women in the car, there wasn't much opportunity to breathe. Looking straight ahead, Rhoda spoke from the corner of her mouth. "Have you ever looked in the little closet next to the women's can?"

"I didn't even know there was a closet there."

"It's almost hidden behind a palm. If management had any brains, they'd make sure it was locked, but they don't."

"Well, what's in there?"

She looked in my eyes and her voice was barely audible. "Toilet paper, towels, soap, light bulbs, window cleaner— all kinds of good stuff." My eyes popped as I realized what she was talking about. She leered at me. "Well, there ought to be some fringe benefits to a job like this."

Florine spoke over her shoulder, "Is it okay with you if we shop first? If there's any time left, we'll grab a hamburger after."

In the store I got a cart and wheeled off down the first aisle. I wanted to get away from Rhoda. I knew she had faults, but a thief? I was so worried I couldn't remember what I wanted to get. Mechanically, I put three cans of dog food in the basket. Should I tell Ellen what Rhoda said, or should I pretend it never happened? Maybe I should stick around after work and tell the custodian. And yet, if the closet was locked the next time Rhoda tried it . . .

As I was walking toward the checkout counter, Florine stopped me. "Where are your Scot Towels?"

"Oh, rats!" I whirled around and practically ran to the paper section.

Lord! What shall I do?

> **"If sinners entice you, do not give in to them. If they say, 'Come along with us . . . we will get all sorts of valuable things . . .' do not go with them" (Prov. 1:10–15).**

Father! You know I wouldn't steal! *Oh, really, Mab?* **But then what about all those company pens in my purse at home? And haven't I used the copy machine many times for myself? In Your eyes I realize that stealing toilet paper is no worse.**

> **"Test me, O Lord, and try me, examine my heart and my mind; for your love is ever before me, and I walk continually in Your truth" (Ps. 26:2–3)**

Father, I don't feel as pure as David did when he wrote this Psalm, but I would like to. Help me to be completely honest with Rhoda—and You.

DILEMMA

BARRICADED BY WORK, I avoided talking to Rhoda the rest of the afternoon, but I couldn't wait to tell my husband the closet tale that night at dinner. He listened intently then asked, "Are you going to tell your boss?"

"I don't know. The woman didn't really say she'd taken anything. You know she'd deny it."

He nodded, frowning. "Yet, I think you should say something to Mr. Ulrich."

"But what if he thinks I'm just jealous of Rhoda? Worried about my job or something?"

He leaned back in his chair, and drew in his breath, then let it out in a rush. "I don't know, honey. It's something you'll have to decide."

At work the next morning, Florine met me in the hall. "Rhoda can't work with you today. I've got a million purchase orders for her to do." I forced myself not to yell *hooray*. "But maybe you two can get together tomorrow."

"Don't worry about it!" I grinned. "She said she already knows my job." Reprieve! I wouldn't have to talk to her this morning. At my desk, however, the grin faded. Did I have a responsibility to "snitch" or not? The Spirit brought to mind the verse, "Anyone, then, who knows the good he ought to do and doesn't do it, sins" (James 4:17). But was talebearing—especially when I didn't have proof—"doing good"?

I had just uncovered my typewriter when Ellen clicked in on spike heels. She handed me an envelope and some bills. "Here are your credentials to get into Convention Center and a hundred bucks. Mr. U. says to buy bunting and whatever else you need to decorate our booth." She lifted an eyebrow. "Don't spend it all in one place." She whirled around to go then looked back. "The trade show is just two days away, so you don't need to come in tomorrow. Just go downtown and be creative."

Walking out to the parking lot, with sunshine cuddling me, I felt like a kid playing hookey. How wonderful to be free! I could shelve my decision about Rhoda for a few days. Yet, like the ugly job of cleaning the oven, I knew that sometime soon I'd have to face it. And for some reason, I was afraid of that woman.

Lord, I don't think Rhoda would hesitate to nail me to the wall to save her own skin. She could probably make them believe I'm the thief.

> **"Do not tremble, do not be afraid . . . Is there any God besides me? No, there is no other Rock . . ." (Isa. 44:8).**

Forgive me, Lord. Sometimes I forget to trust You.

> **"He got up, rebuked the wind and said to the waves, 'Quiet! Be still!' . . . [Then] he said to his disciples, 'Why are you so afraid? Do you still have no faith?' " (Mark 4:39–40).**

I know You'll handle the problem. I just can't figure out how.

CONVENTION TENSION

THE NEXT MORNING on the way downtown, I realized what a blessing it was to live close to the job. The Santa Ana freeway was moving fifteen miles an hour, and the traffic often stopped completely. Besides that, I almost had a wreck when I had to cut across three lanes of traffic to get on the Santa Monica freeway. I let out a sigh when I finally saw the freeway sign, "Convention Center." Although I'd left home this morning at 7:30, it was almost 9:00 when I rolled into the gigantic garage. I parked as close to the entrance as I could because the back seat was filled with stuff I'd have to carry in for our booth.

Loaded down with a a big carton, my purse, and a shopping bag, I started walking. By the time I got to the escalators, I wished I'd worn flats. Pride was the only thing that kept me from crying. I promised myself as soon as I got through carrying in all the supplies, I'd spend the rest of the day in stocking feet. How stupid of me to wear high heels and not even bring a change of shoes.

Inside Yorty Hall, I still had a long way to go to our booth. Some of the displayers were already set up. Their stalls looked smart, professional. Could I do as well? I'd made a banner and a large poster, and they looked okay at home, but how would they look here, in comparison?

I almost stumbled into the space assigned to Vapogas INC, and I plopped the carton and sacks on one of the bare tables. I sank onto one of the chairs and kicked off my shoes. As the pain eased up, I looked around the "cell." It was carpeted in blue, with white dividers—perfect for Vapogas colors of blue and white! I pulled out a corner of blue bunting and smiled. The exact shade! (Lord, did you have this figured out beforehand?)

After a few moments I put on my shoes and stood up. I decided to get that long trek to the car over with.

"You're early!"

I turned so quickly I almost fell. My ears were right. Tanned and splendid, there stood John Beardsley.

Why, Lord? I _prayed_ this wouldn't happen. _Why?_

"Woe to him who quarrels with his Maker . . . Does the clay say to the potter, 'What are you making?' " (Isa. 45:9).

Excuse me, Lord. It's just that I thought I was over it, but he's _magnificent_.

"No temptation has seized you except what is common to man. And God is faithful; he will not let you be tempted beyond what you can bear. But when you are tempted, he will also provide a way out so that you can stand up under it" (1 Cor. 10:13).

BE PREPARED

ALTHOUGH MY HEART seemed to stop when I saw John Beardsley, my mouth was working overtime. "What are *you* doing here?"

He grinned and frowned at the same time. "This is part of Sales."

Stupid question! My face got hot. "Of course." I tried to smile as I picked up my purse. "I have to go back to my car. Lots more stuff to bring in."

"I'll help."

On the way we both tried to be casual, yet I was so aware of his nearness I almost forgot that my feet hurt. I forced myself to remember how disgusting he'd seemed to me at the party, and evidently he was thinking the same thing, because he said, "Mab, I want to apologize for my behavior at the Christmas party. I don't know what got into me." He squinted and grinned one-sidedly. "Well, I do know what got in me. Too much alcohol."

I glanced at him, startled. I saw his jaw muscles work. "That's okay, John. It's forgotten."

"It won't ever be completely forgotten. But that night was a turning point for me." He took a deep breath. "I've joined A. A."

I gawked at him and almost stopped walking. "Alcoholics Anonymous. I didn't realize . . ."

We walked the rest of the way in silence. The flame Satan had tried to rekindle was out. Permanently. The only feeling I had for John now was concern and compassion.

He watched me unlock the car. "Something you said that night keeps bothering me. You said you were a Christian. Isn't everyone born in America a Christian?"

As I looked at him, Lord, I felt a jolt of understanding. I suddenly knew why You had allowed us to work together. I was supposed to witness to him!

"Always be prepared to give an answer to everyone who asks you to give the reason for the hope that you have" (1 Peter 3:15b).

Help! What shall I tell him?

"By this gospel you are saved . . . Christ died for our sins according to the Scriptures . . . He was buried . . . He was raised on the third day" (1 Cor. 15:2–4).

There's a New Testament in the glove compartment. Oh, Lord! Help me find the right Scripture verses.

TRUTH BOOTH

"MY FEET ARE ABSOLUTELY KILLING ME," I moaned when we came back from the car. "I have to take off my shoes."

"Oh, no!" John grinned, holding his nose. "Listen, I'll go get some coffee, and we can talk a little more before we start trimming this place."

While he was gone, I tried to find some Bible verses that would help him understand what it meant to be a Christian. I remembered the 1 Corinthians passage about the body of Christ. Maybe I could read it to him.

"Here you go!" John handed me a cup of coffee. When he saw the New Testament, he said, "I still think being born in the United States makes us Christians."

I kept my finger at chapter 12 and looked at him. "Not really. It's sort of like a woman who doesn't love her husband. She might call herself, Mrs. So-and-So, but her heart isn't in it."

He nodded slightly. "But, there are hundreds of churches—everywhere. Which one's right?"

"The Bible says the true church is people who believe in Jesus. Listen." I began to read: "The body is a unit . . . and though all its parts are many, they form one body. So it is with Christ."

"And you become part of this body just by believing in God?"

"Well, you also have to ask His forgiveness for sins and believe that Jesus paid for them." He drew on the styrofoam cup with his thumbnail. "If you'll read the New Testament, John, you'll find lots of places where it says the church is made up of people like us who believe in Christ." I closed the little book and grinned at him. "The best place to start reading is *you!*"

"Me? What do you mean?"

"*John!* The Gospel of John is the most understandable book in the New Testament."

Thank You for the privilege of being part of Your body. Please help John understand that he needs to believe in You.

"How, then, can they call on the one they have not believed in? And how can they believe in the one of whom they have not heard? And how can they hear without someone preaching to them?" (Rom. 10:14).

What else can I say? I don't want to turn him off.

"For God so loved the world [specifically John] that he gave his one and only Son, that whoever [specifically John] believes in him shall not perish but have eternal life" (John 3:16).

TRUST ME

"HONEY, THANKS FOR making dinner," I cooed. "This meatloaf is delicious."

"How long will you be at the Convention Center?" His voice was petulant.

"Just tomorrow and the next day." I took a big bite and chewed hungrily. "Want you to see my booth. I'm proud of it." He grunted. "All kinds of products on display in other booths—barbecues, camping equipment—there's even a propane potty!" Another grunt. "Where's Joan?"

"Don took her someplace." He gave me a sour look.

"Well, honey, they'll be married in a few months."

"Don't remind me. He acts too familiar with her."

An icicle reached deep inside as I thought of some of the swinging single women in Accounting. "What do you mean?"

"Men are men."

"Don's a Christian!"

"Christian men have the same drives heathen men have."

"We can trust Joan." But doubt snickered at me.

That night I couldn't go to sleep. I got up after midnight and went to the living room. Where was she? At 1:30 I heard Don's car stop at the curb. I waited for about two minutes, then I got up and peeked out. Their heads were together, of course. I felt angry and afraid. What were they doing? What had they done?

At last I heard her key in the door. After a long pause I heard his footsteps receding.

"Mother!" Her eyes were bright with lovelight. "What are you doing up?"

"What are you doing out so late?"

Her face reflected the verbal slap. "We went to a concert."

"I'm sure!" I could feel my mouth pull down.

"Are you accusing me of—"

"Don acts very possessive!"

"But what about me?" Tears filled her eyes. "You don't trust *me!*" She ran down the hall to her room and closed the door.

Oh, Father! What happened? I *do* trust her. Haven't we trained and instructed her about living for You? She's not going to turn from that.

" 'In your anger do not sin.' Do not let the sun go down while you are still angry" (Eph. 4:26).

Joanie, please forgive me, honey. Working in the world and seeing the world's values have warped me.

"Take up the shield of faith, with which you can extinguish all the flaming arrows of the evil one" (Eph. 6:16).

MY TERRITORY

ON THE FREEWAY THIS MORNING I realized that in my anxiety last night, I had forgotten to look up more Scripture verses to show John. Satan certainly had a victory, at least partially. At breakfast, however, Joan said she had forgiven me, and she seemed to be her sunny self. But it's going to take awhile for both of us to quit hurting.

In the Vapogas booth I straightened the stacks of brochures, dumped ashtrays, and threw away coffee cups. I stood in front of the table, admiring a miniature standby gas plant made by one of the draftsmen. The model didn't cover more than two square feet, but it was a perfect representation of a thirty-thousand-gallon fuel tank, a gas mixer, two vaporizers, meters, and hoses. Even the Vapogas INC logo was on all the equipment.

"Pretty ingenious, right?"

I caught my breath and whirled around. "John! If you don't quit sneaking up on me!"

"Hey, you shouldn't have your back to the door. First rule of survival." He chuckled as he opened a sack. "Donuts!"

"Oh, no. You know we'll gain if we eat those."

He bit into one then took two cups of coffee from another sack. "My wife and I talked until two o'clock this morning about religion."

My eyes widened. "You're kidding!"

"I told her everything I could remember that you said, and then we read the whole Gospel of John."

"That's amazing!"

His eyes glowed. "You know, when I first went to Alcoholics Anonymous, I was told that before I could recover, I had to admit that there's a Power greater than myself." He took a lid off his coffee and sipped it. "Well, I'm about convinced that power is Jesus Christ."

I beamed at him, afraid to speak for fear I'd say the wrong thing. Should I invite him to church, or was it too soon?

He took another donut and offered me the sack. "I think my wife and I will start going to church this Sunday."

I almost dropped the sack. "Wonderful! I was just going—"

"My wife's sister has been after us for months to go to her church, so we both figure this is the time."

His wife's sister? Rats! I'm jealous! Wasn't I the one who witnessed to him, Lord? Shouldn't they come to my church?

"Since there is jealousy . . . are you not worldly? . . . For when one says, 'I follow Paul,' and another, 'I follow Apollos,' are you not mere men? . . . I planted the seed, Apollos watered it, but God made it grow" (1 Cor. 3:3b—4, 6).

Father, I wanted the "glory" of introducing them as my trophies. I can't believe I'm still such a carnal Christian.

"The man who plants and the man who waters have one purpose . . . we are God's fellow workers" (1 Cor. 3:8—9).

THE COMPETITION

ON THE LAST DAY of the trade show, John didn't come in because he had to attend a meeting. I had time alone to reflect on God's goodness. One thing I thought was that although I had been disappointed John wouldn't be attending our church, I could see God's protection. There was no denying the attraction between John and me, and while I felt nothing for him now except Christian affection, what might happen inside my deceitful heart if I saw him not only almost everyday at work but at church, too? *Thank You for protecting me, Lord.*

Another thing I realized that day was how I had fallen down in Bible study. When I had tried to talk to John about the Lord, I couldn't always remember a certain verse or where to find it in the Bible. Instead of being a trusty witness, I was a rusty one. *Forgive me, Lord. I promise to get up earlier so I can spend some time alone with you.*

That last day downtown seemed to drag, even though I talked to several people who stopped to look at our display, pick up brochures, or fill out the prospect questionnaire. Late in the afternoon a little man with thin blond hair, Chaplin mustache, plaid sports jacket, and red tie came over and perched on one of our tables. "H'ya, doll." His voice was soft, and he smelled of musk. "How's business?" His name tag read "Nickey Nelson, PETROWAY GAS." Petroway—our biggest competitor.

"Not bad." I tried to look confident as I glanced at the box where we kept the completed questionnaires. "We have a few leads."

"Great!" He stood up, jingling his keys as he moved toward the miniature standby system. "Nice display." While he was studying it, another man stopped at our booth. I talked to him a few moments then turned back to Nickey. I was shocked to see him leafing through the questionnaires in the prospect bag. I picked it up and forced a polite smile. "This isn't on display."

He smirked, stretched, and sauntered toward the aisle. "All's fair in love and war." He winked in a manner I'm sure he thought was irresistible. "Next time we'll try love."

Lord, he's a crook! What a disgusting dork!

"There is no one righteous, not even one . . . All have turned away . . . there is no one who does good, not even one" (Rom. 3:10, 12). "He [the Lord] is patient . . . not wanting anyone to perish, but everyone to come to repentance" (2 Peter 3:9).

Even him, Lord? If judgment was up to me, I'd . . . but then I keep forgetting how tender-hearted You are. After all, You saved even me!

PEACEMAKER

"MOTHER, WANT TO GO TO THE MALL with me tonight?" Joan dumped a stack of books on the coffee table. "Broadway is having a sale on shoes, and I need some to match my going-away suit."

"Well, okay, if daddy doesn't mind." I kissed her on the cheek and breathed in the sweet scent of Wind Song. "I'm sure he won't care if I go."

"Don't be too sure!" Her expression was on the pouty side.

"Still mad at him about the other night?"

"It hurts a lot to know my parents don't trust me." Her tone was indignant, then she patted me. "But I know daddy influenced you. What a grouch!"

"Honey, he's a man. Men see things differently than women do. Especially about other men." She sat down and kicked off her shoes. "Besides, you're his daughter. No man ever thinks a boyfriend is good enough." She flicked a smoldering glance at me. "He does love you, in his quiet way."

She hunched her shoulders. "Oh, I know." Taking a deep breath, she looked up at me. "And I have to admit—but don't tell daddy—sometimes it *is* hard for Don and me not to give in to our feelings. But that's why we double-date and why we pray before we go out and when we come home, too." I bit my lip as I remembered the other night.

When I looked out the window at them, their heads were together. They probably had been praying. She looked up at me with clear-conscience eyes. "Trust me."

"I do. But for the next few weeks, don't do anything that will make daddy or anyone else wonder about you."

"Okay." She grinned as she put her hands on her hips. "But also tell daddy that Don is a fine person and that he's pretty lucky to get him for a son-in-law!"

Will mothers and wives always have to be a bridge between children and fathers?

"Let us therefore make every effort to do what leads to peace" (Rom. 14:19a).

Lord, You know how scary it is to raise children, especially when they get to this stage. Help me say (or not say) the right things.

"Abstain from all appearance of evil" (1 Thess. 5:22 KJV).

LATE!

"I'M SO TIRED THIS MORNING! And my hair won't do anything!" I threw down the comb and plugged in the curling iron. "I'm going to be late!"

"You shouldn't have gone shopping last night," my husband grumped. "When did you finally get to bed, anyway?"

"By the time I got the kitchen cleaned up and took a shower, it was midnight."

"I don't suppose our daughter helped."

I glared at him in the mirror. "She offered, but I told her to shower while I loaded the dishwasher." I rolled a strand of hair around the hot iron. "Honey, don't stay mad. We're not going to have her much longer." Ignoring me, he concentrated on his tie. "She's such a good woman, working four hours a day and taking sixteen units of classwork. When does she have time for anything?"

He put on his coat. "I know. I guess the old man's jealous." He gave me a thin smile and a quick kiss. "See you tonight. If you leave right now, you won't be late."

"Hah!" I looked at myself. I had at least twenty minutes more work to make myself presentable. But though I hurried, I couldn't make headway. Every time I'd roll up a curl, it would plop back down. I got eye shadow on my cheek and had to wash it off. Then I couldn't get the blusher on that cheek to match the other. My skirt was wrinkled, so I had to press it. I kept glancing at the clock and worrying, yet I couldn't seem to finish. My husband was right. I should have stayed home last night, pressed my skirt, and set my hair.

I was only fifteen minutes late, but I felt thirty minutes guilty. I was tiptoeing down the hall when Florine called me in her office. Her boss, Mr. Spencer, and Mr. Ulrich were there as well as Ellen and Rhoda. Everyone had something to say about my tardiness. "Wish I had bankers hours!" "Just getting back from lunch?" "Did you walk to work?"

Mr. Ulrich waited for silence, then he began his oration. "It's unsettling to observe you, Mab, an employee who has been outstanding in many areas, performing in a dilatory manner." He grinned, so I hoped he wasn't really unsettled. But I was determined not to be late again. I was probably the only Bible these people were reading.

Dear Lord, I know being late is no "biggie" to people in the world, but I know it isn't a good Christian example. Actually, it's a form of stealing from the company.

"Don't let anyone look down on you . . . but set an example . . . in speech, in life . . ." (1 Tim. 4:12).

I've almost been late several times. Why is it so hard for me to be on time? Dear Lord, if you were my boss instead of Mr. Ulrich, would I be on time?

Jesus said, "I tell you the truth, whatever you did for one of the least of these . . . you did for me" (Matt. 25:40).

FICA

WHEN THEY WERE THROUGH KIDDING ME about being late, Rhoda said, "I'm glad you showed up. I thought you were going to leave me holding the bag."

My grin stayed in place, but my heart flip-flopped. Had they already caught her stealing? But no one else seemed to notice her remark. Florine said, "It's nice to have you back, even if you were late!" I murmured something and turned to leave. Mr. Ulrich said, "Go into my office, Mab. I'll be right in." *Oh, brother.*

During the two minutes I waited for him, I imagined the worst. They probably had found out about Rhoda and she had implicated me and now Mr. Ulrich was going to fire me. By the time he came in and sat down at his desk, my heart felt like I'd been doing aerobics.

But he was grinning! "Mab, it's my pleasurable task to inform you that you did a meritorious stint at the show. We are in receipt of one purchase order as a consequence and two verisimilar intimations of work forthcoming." I swallowed and smiled. "However, I want to ask you something." *Here it comes.* "Your plans now are to work until the end of May?" I nodded. "On behalf of Vapogas INC I earnestly entreat you to consider the possibility of remaining in our employ. You have become an asset."

I was overwhelmed and pleased. But I didn't want a career. All I wanted was to give Joan a beautiful wedding. "Thank you, Mr. Ulrich. I'll . . . I'll consider it."

In the supply room I began to sort a huge stack of work, mostly purchase orders. Rhoda drifted in and flopped on a chair. Her odor filled the room. "What can I do for you?" I asked, looking at her without smiling.

"Do they ever lay anybody off?" she asked.

"Here? I don't know. Why?" Her eyes narrowed, and she smiled slyly. It made me furious. "Listen, Rhoda," I said, "if you're up to something about that closet, you'd better not involve me. What did you mean about 'being left holding the bag?'"

"The work." She indicated the "In" box. "I'm not doing all that stupid stuff. Just enough to get by." She stood up. "And don't worry about the closet. It's not worth the risk. I have a better plan." She winked and smiled to one side. "They're going to lay *me* off."

"What are you talking about?"

"Unemployment, babe. Unemployment compensation."

Lord, what a conspiring woman! At least she's abandoned the closet caper. But what nerve, planning to get wages for not working!

"These . . . lie in wait for their own blood; they waylay only themselves! Such is the end of all who go after ill-gotten gain; it takes away the lives of those who get it" (Prov. 1:18–19).

Thank You, Lord, that I don't have to make waves about the supply closet, but now what is my responsibility?

"Remember this: Whoever turns a sinner away from his error will save him from death and cover over a multitude of sins" (James 5:20).

HEM-HAW HANDMAID

WHEN THE HOLY SPIRIT pointed out that verse about turning a sinner away from his error, I cringed. I could just imagine myself telling Rhoda about Jesus and the cross! My cheeks felt hot when I visualized her sneering expression.

Lord, couldn't you get Betty to speak to her? It would be right down her alley. I mean, Rhoda's a real pagan.

"You remember Joshua, don't you?" the Lord seemed to say.

Yes, Lord, but—

"And what did I tell him?"

You said to be strong and courageous—

"That's right. I never left him, and I will never leave you."

Pagan was just walking out the door. "Rhoda! Wait a minute." I grabbed my purse and pulled out a dog-eared salvation tract. "Here's something!"

Frowning, she stepped back into the room. "What's this?"

"Uh, it tells how, well, on the back there, uh, is our church address, if you ever want to come." I smiled winningly, although one side of my mouth trembled. "And, uh, it has a little message about how to find, uh, peace."

"Peace?" One eyebrow raised. "I already know how." She lifted her hand as if she were holding a glass. "And, frankly, churches turn me off. But thanks. I'll read it."

How was that, Lord?

"Not what I had in mind. But it will do, for starters."

Lord, I feel as if I'd rather be whipped than try to talk to Rhoda about my faith. I guess I fear her ridicule—or wrath.

"Be merciful to those who doubt; snatch them from the fire . . . show mercy . . ." (Jude 22, 23).

But it's hard to be merciful toward some people, Lord. Why did she ever have to cross my path? At least I gave her a tract. That should free me from responsibility. Shouldn't it?

"Though I am free and belong to no man, I make myself a slave to everyone, to win as many as possible" (1 Cor. 9:19).

ACCUSED

IN THE LUNCHROOM, glancing over my shoulder to be sure that only Florine and Ellen were there, I asked, "What are the rules about unemployment compensation?"

Florine looked at me. "Are you planning to get laid off?"

"I hope not!"

"No chance," Ellen rasped. "Didn't you know Mr. U. wants her to keep working?" I glanced at Ellen. That was sarcasm in her voice.

"So why do you want to know about unemployment?" Florine asked.

"Well . . ." I took a deep breath. "I feel like a traitor if I tell and a traitor if I don't."

"Come on, Mab." Ellen's tone was sharp. "Anyone with all your skills can speak plainer than that." Again I looked at her, and this time her hostile eyes met mine. Unsettled, I stuttered slightly. "It's, uh, just that, she—Rhoda—is planning to get laid off so she can draw unemployment."

Both women looked dumfounded, then Ellen made a whispered remark about Rhoda's probable off-hours occupation.

"Can she do that?" I asked. "I mean, just deliberately act in a way so Mr. U. will lay her off?"

"If he has to write her up with a couple of warnings about poor work, then she won't be able to draw unemployment."

Florine lit a cigarette, and smoke billowed out around our heads. "She does a good job, at least so far."

"I did quite a bit of her work this morning." I really felt like a traitor now. Was this the way to win Rhoda to the Lord?

Ellen frowned at me. "Listen, you're supposed to be doing my work, not Florine's. Why do you think we hired Rhoda?"

I bit the edge of my lip. "I just didn't want to make waves."

Ellen's thin lips turned down. "Or did you want to prove how indispensable you are?"

"Hey, what's wrong, Ellen?" I countered. "Why are you mad at me?"

"Excuse me!" Florine jumped up, wadded up her sack, and tossed it in the waste basket on her way out. "Back to work."

Ellen watched her go then turned on me. Her eyes were hard and enormous behind thick glasses. "Now that you bring it up, I don't appreciate you kissing up to Mr. Ulrich. I still have three years before retirement, and I don't want you taking over my job."

I was stunned, Lord. And even more unusual for me, I was speechless.

"Then Pilate asked him, 'Don't you hear how many things they are accusing you of?' But Jesus made no reply, not even to a single charge—to the great amazement of the governor" (Matt. 27:13–14).

My silence had nothing to do with being Christlike. I just couldn't think of anything to say. And, Lord, what have I done that would seem like "kissing up"?

> "Blessed are you when people insult you, persecute you and falsely say all kinds of evil against you . . . be glad, because great is your reward in heaven" (Matt. 5:11–12a).

I don't feel very glad. I feel more like crying.

INCONVENIENT INVASION

AT 5:00 I COULDN'T WAIT TO RUSH HOME and tell my family about my rotten day, but a letter from friends made me forget the office.

"Dear Ones," it read. "Keith has five weeks vacation this year, so the four of us, Keith, Chad, my sister's boy, and I are going to see America! We'll be in Los Angeles four days and hope we can spend it with you. Rob is 17 and Chad is 15, so they'll be good company for each other and can share the same bed. If you don't have room, reserve motel accommodations, okay? We should arrive the afternoon of the twelfth."

The twelfth . . . *this* Friday! I closed my eyes and fell over on the couch. When I opened them, all I could see was one dusty thing after another. I hadn't thoroughly cleaned the house since I started to work. How could I bear to have my girlhood friend see this mess? We had stayed at their house several times, and I remembered that Vicki was such a good housekeeper. "Why did you decide to come now?" I mumbled. "Didn't I write you at Christmas that I'm working? With Joan getting married in two months, I don't have time to entertain anyone!" Half sobbing, I went to the kitchen and put on a pot of coffee. All the woodwork would have to be scrubbed. And the stove was revolting! The refrigerator. Yuk. I wouldn't even let my mother see it, much less house guests. Both bathrooms looked as if they belonged in a flophouse. How could normal, reasonably clean people get things so filthy?

Standing beside an unmade bed, I kicked a pair of shoes under the spread. "Dear Lord, it's not a convenient time for guests. Would you please make them change their minds?"

"Hast thou forgotten?" (Is that You, Lord?) "Your friends are not yet believers. This is My plan to let them hear and see the good news in action."

The family rallied to the fight. Ron shampooed carpets, my husband mowed, watered, and did some outside painting. Joan and I scrubbed woodwork, washed windows, and cleaned every appliance in the kitchen. By staying up late, drinking lots of coffee and Pepsi, and eating most of our meals out, by Friday our house was presentable. For sleeping arrangements, Ron said he could stay with a buddy on campus, and Joan said she didn't mind sleeping on the couch.

Vicki later hugged me. "You make us feel so welcome."

"You *are* welcome!" Was that a lie? No. I honestly meant it.

I would never have believed we could have gotten so much done in three days.

Thanks for Your help, Lord. It's great to have things clean again, and I love Vicki. But I still say that right now is an inconvenient time to sit around visiting and sightseeing.

"And God is able to make *all* grace abound to you, so that in *all* things at *all* times, having *all* that you need, you will abound in every good work" (2 Cor. 9:8, italics added).

Thanks for not letting me send them to a motel, Lord.

A BETTER PLAN

"WELCOME BACK!" MITZI CALLED as soon as I walked in on Tuesday morning. "What did you do while your company was here?"

"Dishes!" I flopped on a chair in the lobby and smiled.

"I can imagine. Florine said an army from back East invaded."

"Just four, and actually we ate out quite a bit. But with eight people around, somebody was always hungry. Anyway, we had a good time. First night they were here we went to Knott's Berry Farm."

"I love Knott's!"

"It was fun. Then Saturday we went to Disneyland."

"Good! They say there are a lot of new attractions."

"We were there from eleven o'clock in the morning until after the evening fireworks, and I don't think we saw everything. We were pooped!"

Mitzi's eyes danced with challenge. "I'll bet you didn't go to church Sunday!"

I had told her once that unless I was sick or there was some other urgent reason, I went to church every Sunday. Now she was testing me! I bit my lip as I remembered Saturday night. We all had been so tired that I had decided not to invite them to church and just relax. But Sunday morning I awoke in plenty of time to get ready, and when I went to the kitchen to make coffee, Vicki was already there and dressed.

"Yes, I went to church." I took a deep breath. That was close. I stood up and started toward the hall. I looked back at her. "The men stayed home, but Vicki and the boys went with me. Hey, your mouth's open!" I grinned at her. "Then yesterday we got up early and drove to Tiajuana to see a bull fight! It was awful! I never—"

"You know . . ." Mitzi's eyes were soft, "I'd like to go to church with you, too. Sometime."

Now my mouth was open. When I recovered I said, "How about next Sunday?"

She looked away. "I'll let you know."

Lord, what if I hadn't awakened in time Sunday? Mitzi fully expected me to skip church, and I intended to, but You had a better plan.

> **"Let us not give up meeting together, as some are in the habit of doing, but let us encourage one another—and all the more as you see the Day approaching" (Heb. 10:25).**

Strange and exciting! First John Beardsley, then Rhoda, now Mitzi. I'm beginning to get the feeling You had more in mind than Joan's wedding when You let me get this job.

> **"In everything set them an example by doing what is good" (Titus 2:7a).**

COUNTING THE DAYS

THE ANTICIPATION I FELT ABOUT MITZI going to church faded as I walked down the hall toward Ellen's office. I hated to see her. Although I had tried to convince her that day at lunch that I did not want a career, and certainly not her job, she hadn't relaxed very much. The old grumbler. She reminded me of one of my aunts who said she'd rather stay mad than make up.

At Florine's door I paused to say hello, but the word died before I got it out. Rhoda was sitting at her desk in a faded blue mumu, with her hair up on pink rollers. Her back was to me, and I didn't see Florine, so I slipped on by without speaking.

Florine, her eyes wide with indignation, was in Ellen's office. "Her work is okay," she was saying, "and we don't have a dress code, so what can I do?"

Ellen hunched her skinny shoulders. "I don't know. Mr. U. won't be in until about eleven o'clock, but I know he won't put up with that."

"Hi, Mab." Florine's smile was weak. "Glad you're back."

Ellen didn't echo that remark. Instead she gave me a cold look and a stack of letters. "These have to be coded and filed. I assumed I was still on her list.

In my little office I looked at the desk calendar. Five more weeks, and I would be home free, literally! I couldn't wait. I was glad that I had the ability to earn money, that I could take care of myself if necessary. But I was looking forward to being a homemaker again—studying the Bible as long as I wanted in the mornings, keeping up the house and our clothes, working in the flower beds, helping in Vacation Bible School. Most of all I was looking forward to being away from Ellen. It really hurt to know that she thought I was somewhat less than adorable. My last day couldn't come soon enough.

I was tempted, Lord, to let Ellen think I *might* take her job, just because she's been so mean to me, the old frog. But I decided to tell Mr. Ulrich today that May 30th definitely will be my last day.

"Do not repay anyone evil for evil. Be careful to do what is right in the eyes of everybody" (Rom. 12:17).

Ellen *thinks* she's jealous and afraid of me because I'm younger, but I realize it's the same old battle—the Spirit of God versus the spirit of the world.

"Do not be overcome by evil, but overcome evil with good" (Rom. 12:21).

Give me grace to be a good testimony.

SHOWERS OF DRESSING

ALL THE REST OF THE DAY Ellen and I spoke only when necessary. I was peeved and worked as hard as I could. However, by the time I got home, I had cooled down. I even tried to think of some way I could win back her friendship. Joan came in before I could think of a plan.

"The kids at school are giving me a shower!" Her tone of voice and the light in her eyes reminded me of a day when she was nine and had bounded in the front door yelling, "I've been invited to a birthday party!" My heart hurt. This baby was about to fly away.

"That's wonderful, honey." I blinked fast. "My goodness, you already had a church shower—"

"I know! But this is going to be a personal shower."

The night of the party Don's mom and I sat together in a circle of metal chairs in one of the buildings at Biola. We watched all the darling co-eds (some of them still wobbly on spike heels) giggling, combing their hair, touching up their make-up, hugging Joan. Quite a few gifts were piled on a table, and a huge, beautifully wrapped box was on the floor beside it.

Deanna, one of Joan's close friends, handed out paper and pencils for a game—something about items one could take on a honeymoon. It took a long time, and of course someone got first prize, and someone got the booby prize. After a lot of giggling and talking, Joan finally was allowed to open her presents.

What a beautiful selection of lingerie! Full slips, half-slips, bouffant nighties, lace-trimmed bras and panties. I was so happy for my Joanie. Of course each gift had to be passed around the room for touching and inspection. I glanced at my watch. This was taking longer than I had expected. It would be hard to get up in the morning.

Now the girls were teasing Joan about the big box. "I can't imagine what's in it!" She walked around it, shaking her head.

"Open it! Hurry up!" I heard myself above the other voices.

Slowly, with a puzzled smile on her face, she tore off the paper and opened the lid, revealing wads of white tissue paper. She carefully lifted out the top layer. "Feels warm! You guys! This better not be a puppy!" She reached down in the box, her eyes grew round, then she screamed.

Out jumped Don! Everyone howled with laughter. Then with a piece of tissue she wiped the perspiration from his face and kissed him, while all of us crooned, "A-w-w-w!"

Poor Don! For at least an hour his six-foot frame had been folded up in that box. What love he must have for my daughter to be willing to go along with that gag!

For some reason, Lord, I thought of You. How You must love us, to go through what You did.

"This is how we know what love is: Jesus Christ laid down his life for us" (1 John 3:16b).

Dear God, as Joan responds to Don's love, help me to respond to Your love.

"Dear children, let us not love with words or tongue but with actions and in truth" (1 John 3:18).

MISSION ACCOMPLISHED

INSTEAD OF FEELING TIRED the morning after Joan's shower, I felt exhilarated. It must have been all those satiny, soft garments. I had never bought expensive lingerie for myself, but I was glad for Joan to start her marriage with so many pretty things. The women in the church also had given her a bountiful shower. Everything seemed to be working out for Joan's wedding day. Although I would only be receiving three more pay checks, almost everything was paid for. The flowers, invitations, tuxedos, and refreshments. I kept grinning all the way to work.

I was humming when I went into Ellen's office, and she seemed more like her old self. I was sure Mr. Ulrich had told her I had definitely resigned and wouldn't be around after the end of the month.

She gave me a tight smile. "Florine said your daughter had another shower last night."

"Yes . . ." I grinned. "Mostly beautiful undies."

"Oh?" She leered. "Anything like what's in Florine's office?"

"Huh? What's up?"

"Go take a peek."

Stealthily, I eased over to Florine's office and looked. There was Rhoda, this time in short shorts and halter, with her hair in stubby braids.

Back in Ellen's office I closed my eyes and shook my head. "What's going to happen?"

"Mr. Ulrich is going to lay her off. He'd rather have her go on unemployment than fight a hearing."

About eleven o'clock Rhoda came swaggering and smirking into the supply room. She waved a slip of paper under my nose. "Ol' Useless Ulrich laid me off! Twenty-six weeks I don't have to worry about working for a living! Whoopee!" She threw back her head and cackled. "I feel so good you might even see me in church!"

Oh, Lord, I'm not ready for that! I would hate to have people at church think she was my friend.

"As believers in our glorious Lord Jesus Christ, don't show favoritism" (James 2:1).

Ouch! I'm sorry, Lord. I keep forgetting what a disgusting person I was before You saved me. But Rhoda? If she does come to church, You'll have to give me *megagrace*.

"God our Savior . . . wants all men to be saved and to come to a knowledge of the truth" (1 Tim. 2:3b–4).

THE IN GROUP

"MITZI, DO YOU THINK IT WOULD BE OKAY to put this on the bulletin board in the lunchroom?" I gave her one of Joan's wedding invitations. "Or do you think I should send one to every employee?"

She looked wise. "Depends on how many gifts you want her to get."

"That's just it. Most of these people don't know me or Joan. But if they get an invitation, they'd feel obligated."

She nodded. "You can send invitations to the people you know well, like me. Then go ahead and put one on the bulletin board. That way no one can feel snubbed or pressured."

"Mitzi, you're so intelligent! I'll bet you'll be president of the company some day."

"Of course!" She read the invitation then looked up, frowning. "I never saw that before."

"What?"

She put her finger on the third line and read aloud. "'. . . request the honor of your presence at the marriage in Christ of their daughter.' What does 'in Christ' mean?"

"Let's see. How can I explain it?" I thought a moment. "In one of the Gospels, Jesus said that He was the Vine. You know, like the main part of a grapevine. And that those who believe in Him are branches. I guess the symbolism is that the life-giving substance that's in the main vine is also in the branches." I lifted my hand and let it fall in my lap. "I think 'in Christ' is another way of saying 'in God's family.'"

Her eyes narrowed as she held my gaze a moment. "I know your family is religious, but is your daughter's fiancé religious?"

I smiled as I thought of my teasing, joking, future son-in-law. "I don't think any of us are *religious*. But, yes, Don believes he is a sinner and that Jesus Christ is his Savior."

"*That* sounds pretty religious to me!"

I wrinkled my nose. "I know. No matter how you talk about faith, it usually comes out sounding 'holier-than-thou.' I don't mean for it to. True faith is so simple—"

"Well, whatever." She seemed tired of the conversation. "Anyway, you can count on me at the nuptials! I'll even dance on the table if you want me to!"

I hope my explanation of what it means to be "in Christ" didn't drive Mitzi further away. I was only trying to say what You said.

"I am the vine; you are the branches. If a man remains in me and I in him, he will bear much fruit; apart from me you can do nothing" (John 15:5).

Lord Jesus, please save Mitzi. Then she'll understand "in Christ" because *she'll* be in You, too.

"If you remain in me and my words remain in you, ask whatever you wish, and it will be given you" (John 15:7).

LOVE NEST

"MOTHER! DON AND I have found an apartment! You've got to come see it!"

"In these old pants?" I closed the lid on the washing machine and stepped over a pile of dirty clothes.

"Sure! Nobody will see you. It's just ten minutes from here. Isn't that wonderful?"

I was glad to get away from my thoughts that Saturday morning. I had faced up to how rotten I was about not wanting Rhoda to come to our church, but I still hadn't reached the place of true repentance . . . inviting her.

As we sped along in Joan's old Plymouth, she told me the details. The rent was right, the apartment was close to college, and the only drawback was that it was upstairs with no air conditioning.

"That won't kill you, honey. We don't have air conditioning."

"But we don't have an upstairs, either."

It was pretty warm in their tiny, three-room apartment, even though it was only May. "But it's so clean!" I cheered. "New carpeting!"

"I know." Joan's expression was a mixture of pride and wonder. "Our landlady is nice, too. Oh, mother! Isn't it cute? I know the Lord led us to it."

The following Saturday they began to move in. "Don, you can have my daughter's hand in marriage," Joan's dad declared, "providing you take her piano, too."

Don threw his arm over his face. "Oh, no! The wedding is off!" But with the help of his dad, brother, and a friend, he tussled the old upright up the stairs. I helped Joan put in shelf paper, wash new dishes, fold new towels, and put new sheets on the bed. By the end of the day their apartment was ready for occupancy. Alone in the tiny bathroom, tears splashed in the wash basin while I prayed.

Lord, bless this house, bless Joan and Don. May they always live for You.

    "Unless the Lord build the house, its builders labor in vain" (Ps. 127:1a).

They love you now, dear Lord. May they always want You to be the head of their home.

    "Those who trust in the Lord are like Mount Zion, which cannot be shaken but endures forever" (Ps. 125:1).

Into Your hands, O Lord, I give my little girl.

WINDING DOWN

"THEY TELL ME THIS IS YOUR LAST DAY," Valorie Vasquez said in her rich Mexican voice. "We'll miss you!"

"Well, thank you!" Would I miss them? I didn't think so. I felt like a horse running for the stable. I couldn't wait to be a homemaker again.

"We're taking Mab to lunch at the bowling alley," Florine said. "Why don't you come, too?"

"I'd like to, but Mr. Archibald is out of town. I can't leave."

I shook my head. "That's the price you pay for being at the top."

At the bowling alley Mitzi had decorated a table with strips of crepe paper, and the chair at the head had a sign, "Bye-bye, Mab."

There was a gift, too, and a card signed by just about everyone.

"Now order whatever you want on the menu," Florine whispered.

"Yeah!" Mitzi added. "But not over a buck."

"Open your present!" Myrna called. I remembered the day she had collected for Mitzi's birthday. Would there be black undies for me? And if so, would they expect me to model! Inside was a soft, white silk blouse, with yards of delicate lace! I loved it. My throat felt tight, and I bit my lip. Maybe I *would* miss this bunch. I looked around the table: irrepressible Mitzi, maybe closer to "the kingdom" now than when I first met her; down-with-pagans-Betty, a sincere Christian who was more devoted to Christ than I; Florine and Ellen, unsaved and set in their ways, but I would keep praying; and Myrna, who just needed someone to love her and Jesus did. *Keep praying for all of them, Mab.* As I looked around at each one, there were tears in my eyes. "Thank you! Thank you so much! And listen, this isn't goodbye, okay? I'll see you at the wedding."

Lord, please save Florine, Ellen, Mitzi, and Myrna. Help me, even this last day, to give out Your message.

> **Jesus said, "My prayer is not for them [believers] alone. I pray also for those who will believe in me through their message, that all of them may be one, Father, just as you are in me and I am in you" (John 17:20–21).**

I haven't been very wise or very brave these past months. Forgive me, Lord, for not speaking out for You as much as I could have.

> **"He who wins souls is wise" (Prov. 11:30).**

NERVES

"HOW'S THE LADY OF LEISURE?" my husband asked the first Monday evening after I was through working at Vapogas INC.

"Antsy!" I shook my head and sighed. "I don't know what's the matter, but I can't relax. I thought I'd go back to bed after you left—or at least take a nap, and I didn't do either."

"Well, at least it smells good in here. What's cookin'?"

"Pot roast. Carrots and stuff."

"Wonderful! I see you watered, too."

"I couldn't stay quiet. I guess I'm worrying."

"Worrying? About the wedding?"

"Only twelve days to get this house clean and the yard nice. I have to set out some new flowers—"

"Hold it! Why do we have to have everything so jazzed up here? The reception is at church."

"Yes, but Sis is coming down a couple of days before the wedding, and the maid of honor will be here overnight. I want things pretty."

"Always something! Why couldn't Joan have accepted the money I offered her to elope!"

"Don't tell me you're not excited about walking down the aisle in a tuxedo, with your beautiful daughter on your arm?" He gave me a noncommittal stare. "I know you are! I'm looking forward to wearing my new blue dress." I grinned at him. "And shoes and hat to match. But I can't help but worry something will go wrong at the wedding!" I gasped. "Oh! I almost forgot! I told the florist you could build a little thing for the kids to kneel on. He was going to charge an awful price to rent one."

His mouth opened. "Build one?"

"It won't be that hard, will it? Here, I'll draw a picture." I sketched a simple kneeling bench and gave it to him. "When you get it done, I'll cover it with foam rubber and white satin."

He closed his eyes a second. "Okay. I'll try to do it next weekend."

"Next weekend? Oh, please make it tonight! Otherwise I'll worry."

I know I'm not supposed to worry, Lord, and I'm trying to rest in You, but it's awfully hard when your only daughter is having a church wedding.

Jesus said, "Who of you by worrying can add a single hour to his life?" (Luke 12:25). "Trust in the Lord with all your heart and lean not on your own understanding; in all your ways acknowledge him, and he will make your paths straight" (Prov. 3:5—6).

Okay, Lord. I'll try to relax. But how am I going to know what things I'm supposed to take care of and what things You'll handle?

TOASTERS—ABUNDANTLY ABOVE

"IT'S OVER!" Joan sang out as the screen door banged. Alarmed, I hurried from the kitchen. "What's over?"

"School! I'm free!"

"Whew! You scared me. I thought you meant you and Don."

"Oh, mother! We'll never break up. The Lord brought us together, and He'll keep us together 'until death do us part.'" She hugged me. "I'm hungry."

"Before we have lunch, open your presents!"

Her eyes widened. "More presents?"

I pointed to three packages United Parcel Service had delivered that morning. She dropped her purse, grabbed a package, and began to pull at the tape.

"Wait! You'll wreck your nails. I'll get a knife."

She sliced the tape neatly, took an envelope from the gift inside, and sat down on the couch to read it. "It's from Bob T-Tsuji."

I drew in my breath. "Accounting! I didn't even send him an invitation."

"Look! It's beautiful! Stainless tableware!'

"I can't believe he'd buy such an expensive gift. I hardly knew him."

With eyes sparkling, she put the tableware aside and picked up a square box. "This is heavy. It's from a Mr. and Mrs. H. McCormick."

"That's Mitzi! You know, the switchboard operator."
Joan yanked open the flaps of the box. "Wow! An
electric fry pan!"

"My goodness!" I frowned as I shook my head. "She
shouldn't have spent that much." I handed the last gift to
Joan. "This is from Mr. Ulrich, my former boss."

Joan cut the tape and looked in. "Oh, no!" She began
to chuckle. "Not another one!"

"What?"

Her chuckling turned to laughter, and finally she fell
back against the couch, holding her stomach, near
hysteria. "What (ho, ho) are we (hee, hee) going to do
(ha ha) with four toasters?"

I laughed too. "Make a lot of toast!"

She pulled it out of the gift box. "But isn't it beautiful!"

"Joanie, be sure to send thank you notes to these people.
They know we're Christians, and I want us to be a good
testimony."

"I will. I'll do it this afternoon." She began to chuckle
again. "I need a photocopied form letter: 'Thank you for
the toaster'!"

I'm stunned that the people at Vapogas would give Joan
such expensive gifts. It must be your doing, Lord.

"The Lord . . . made the Egyptians favorably disposed
toward the people and they gave them . . . [silver and
gold]" (Exod. 12:35–36).

It thrills me to see Joan and Don receive so many nice
things. I know they aren't perfect, Lord, but they're trying
to walk with you.

"For the Lord God is a sun and shield . . . no good thing will he withhold from them that walk uprightly" (Ps. 84:11 KJV).

SISSIE'S SONG

"I'M SO GLAD JOHNNY WAS WILLING to let you come down for the wedding, Dena!" I hugged my sister, amazed that we were looking more alike with every passing year. She was shorter, but we both had blue-green eyes, pug noses, wide mouths, and brown hair.

"Well!" She put her hands on her hips. "I couldn't stand not seeing my favorite niece get married!" Her grin was impish. "Anyway, it's been too long since you and I had a hot fudge sundae together!"

At lunch Dena asked Joan questions about the wedding, and naturally Joan was delighted to talk about it, since that's all she was thinking about anyway. "Do you have a soloist?" Dena asked.

Joan beamed. "Oh, yes! He's the neatest guy, one of Don's best friends."

Dena looked down, rearranged her napkin, then moved a potato chip around on her plate. I could see she was struggling to keep from crying.

"What's wrong?" My voice was too loud.

There were big tears in her eyes. "Nothing . . . It's just . . . I thought Joan would want me to sing at her wedding."

Joan and I looked at each other, dismayed and embarrassed. I didn't know about Joan, but I had completely forgotten my sister had a good voice and often sang in her own church.

"Oh, Sissie!" Joan reached out to pat her shoulder. "I'm so sorry! I . . . I just didn't think . . ."

Dena waved away her explanation. "It's all right." She forced herself to smile. "I know I'm getting old."

"No you're not!" Joan hugged her. "It's just that Don and I planned everything together, and . . ." She lifted her hands, with a sad expression on her face.

I felt sad, too, and sorry. Why was I so thoughtless? It would have made my sister feel important and happy to be asked to sing. At least I could have suggested it to Joan.

Lord, my sister looked so hurt, so left out.

"Be kind and compassionate to one another" (Eph. 4:32a).

Lord, I'm so sorry Joan and I didn't include Dena in the wedding plans. Please take away her sad feelings. Help me to be kinder, more thoughtful, more concerned for others.

"Each of you should look not only to your own interests, but also to the interests of others" (Phil. 2:4).

IST DIS DER DAY?

DENA CAME OUT OF THE HOUSE SMILING. "I just talked to Johnny. Honestly, I think his accent is getting worse! 'Ist dis der vedding day?' " she mimicked fondly. "He said he'd be praying for us."

My husband looked harried and ignored her remark. There were tiny beads of sweat on his forehead. "You're sure everything is in the car?"

"I'm sure!" Joan patted his arm. "Never fear, daddy!"

From the porch step I watched them as if in a dream. All of us, including Dena and Joan's maid of honor, had showered, shampooed, and done our very best with hair, faces, and nails. But since Joan and I would put on our wedding clothes at church, we were dressed casually. Joan was in jeans and T-shirt, and I looked bizarre in a faded print, tennis shoes, and my wedding hat.

"Why did you put on your hat?" Joan teased.

"Because I was afraid it would get smashed in the car. Look in there."

At the church Don's mom was already setting up the four-tiered cake. She was nervous and near tears. "One of the layers broke! I don't know if I can patch it up or not."

Our church friends had done a good job decorating the fellowship hall. It looked like loveland, with pink and white streamers, bells, flowers, and skirted tablecloths.

In the old sanctuary, a white canvas runner stretched to the platform, where two seven-branched candelabra flanked the one large candle that represented Christ. Our homemade, satin kneeling bench looked fine between two huge baskets of white mums and gladiolus blossoms.

The church hostess arrived and took charge: all the women in the nursery, all the men in the pastor's study. Trembling inside, I watched Joan's giggling bridesmaids help her dress. From time to time I peeked out from behind the drapes. "People are starting to arrive," I rasped. "There's my boss!"

The photographer came, bringing Joan's dad. "Bride, give your dad a nice kiss." Then the photographer took pictures of her garter, the bridesmaids, individually and in groups. He took so many pictures I was afraid he'd make us late for the ceremony. "Now, mother, one with daughter. Adjust her veil. There, that's (flash) perfect!"

"The ushers are taking in the grandmas!" my husband warned.

For the last time I kissed my unmarried daughter then went out to meet the usher. *The church is packed!*

Is that the wedding march the organist is playing? Yes! Time for my big part. I stood, turned around, and smiled. Every eye was on me. Then, as one, the crowd stood and turned to look at Joan. I'd never seen any bride anywhere as starlit, luminous, and pristinely beautiful as my baby! She took my breath away! But I didn't cry.

"The ring, a symbol of your everlasting love and of eternity . . ."

"In sickness and in health . . ,"

"Forsaking all others . . ."

"Until death do you part . . ."

"Pronounce you husband and wife . . ."

"Ladies and gentlemen, I introduce to you, Mr. and Mrs. Donald Clucas!"

Don, my son! Take care of this child. She's almost a woman, but she's still such a . . . such an airhead.

Lord Jesus, please. Don't let them ever, ever, ever, separate, much less divorce.

"For this reason a man will leave his father and mother and be united to his wife, and they will become one flesh" (Gen. 2:24). "They are no longer two, but one. Therefore what God has joined together, let man not separate" (Mark 10:8b-9).

BITS AND PIECES

AT THE RECEPTION . . .

"Mr. Ulrich! I'm so pleased that you and Mrs. Ulrich could come!"

"My dear, we want to convey our sincere gratitude for the opportunity to witness this superb ceremony of avouchment. Most profound."

"Thank you for coming, Betty.

"It was precious! Maybe what your preacher said will reach some of these pagans . . ."

"What did you say, honey?"

"I said, 'Will this line never end?' I want to go home . . ."

"John Beardsley!"

"You're as radiant as the bride! By the way, this is the first wedding I've ever been to that didn't serve booze. That's terrific!"

"Hello, my dearest Sis."

"Did you know over four hundred people are here? I'm glad now that Joan didn't ask me to sing!"

"I'm glad you could make it, Florine."

"I wouldn't have missed it! No wonder you wanted to work for this. And we still need you! Sure you won't come back?"

"Ellen! I didn't know you were coming."

"Florine offered to pick me up. I've never been to a wedding that was so real, instead of ritual."

"Hey, Myrna. How are you doing?"

"My feet hurt. Can you see where I had to patch the cake? Thank goodness I brought extra frosting."

"Mitzi-babe! Oops. I'm sorry. I got lipstick on your cheek."

"This wedding was so beautiful I can't quit crying!"

"Honey, did you know the kids are leaving as soon as they cut the cake?"

"You mean we have to take all those gifts home? I'll never forgive that kid for not eloping . . ."

"Thanks for everything, Mab."

"Don! That's the first time you ever kissed me!"

"Joanie . . ."

"Mother, I love you! How can I ever thank you for all you've done?"

And dear Lord, how can I ever thank You for all You've done? You've taken care of everything.

"He tends his flock like a shepherd: He gathers the lambs in his arms and carries them close to his heart" (Isa. 40:11a).

Dear Jesus, how I wish all the people at Vapogas could realize how much You love every one of them.

"For there is no difference between Jew and Gentile— the same Lord is Lord of all and richly blesses all who call on him, for, 'Everyone who calls on the name of the Lord will be saved' " (Rom. 10:12–13).